Creative, sustainable designs
for the twenty-first century

GREEN DESIGN

Marcus Fairs foreword by **Tom Dixon**

North Atlantic Books
Berkeley, California

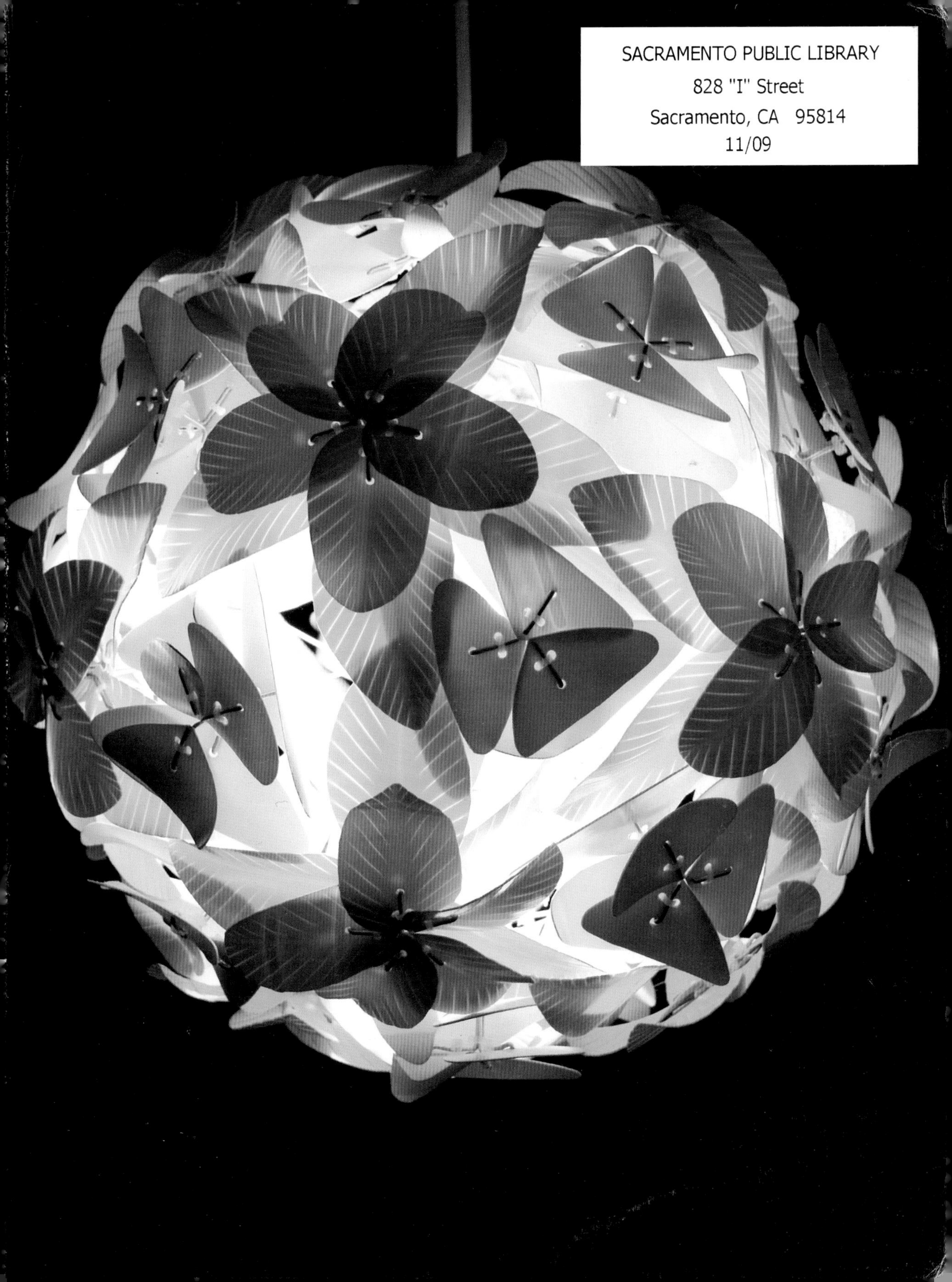

For Jordi and Millie

Published by

Carlton Books Limited	and	North Atlantic Books
20 Mortimer Street		P. O. Box 12327
London W1T 3JW		Berkeley, California 94712

Book design by Barbara Zuñiga. Cover design by Suzanne Albertson.
Printed in Dubai

Green Design: Creative Sustainable Designs for the Twenty-First Century is sponsored by the Society for the Study of Native Arts and Sciences, a nonprofit educational corporation whose goals are to develop an educational and cross-cultural perspective linking various scientific, social, and artistic fields; to nurture a holistic view of arts, sciences, humanities, and healing; and to publish and distribute literature on the relationship of mind, body, and nature.

North Atlantic Books' publications are available through most bookstores. For further information, visit our Web site at www.northatlanticbooks.com or call 800-733-3000.

Library of Congress Cataloging-in-Publication Data

Fairs, Marcus.
 Green design : creative sustainable designs for the twenty-first century / Marcus Fairs ; foreword by Tom Dixon.
   p. cm.
 Includes bibliographical references and index.
 ISBN 978-1-55643-836-3 (alk. paper)
 1. Sustainable design. 2. Design—History—21st century. 3. Design, Industrial—History—21st century. I. Title. II. Title: Creative sustainable designs for the twenty-first century.
 NK1520.F35 2009
 745.2--dc22

           2009003848

1 2 3 4 5 6 7 8 9 ORIENTAL PRESS 14 13 12 11 10 09

Contents

Foreword

Green design has become one of the most debated topics in the media, among the most discussed in politics, the most mentioned in education, and the most fiercely defended by all manner of interest groups, but still remains the most confusing of subjects for the layperson—and certainly still remains a mystery to most consumers. And that confusion extends to the design community and beyond, where it proves increasingly difficult to marry up the twin demands of encouraging consumption while at the same time reducing environmental impact.

The increasing noise around the subject adds to the confusion, where marketing companies vie with each other to convince us that one oil and fuel giant is greener than the other, that by buying this car rather than that one we are being more sustainable, and

governments put out conflicting messages, on one side promoting growth, increased wealth, and consumption as the imperative, while simultaneously pointing out the dire state of the world on the other.

Personally, despite having spent an amount of time and energy on exploring the subject, I still cannot claim to have reached any degree of clarity in terms of understanding the complexity of the subject, and have yet to find a way to digest all the different disciplines, contradictory opinions, opposing statistics, and hysteria that surround the subject.

My input into the debate has been to focus on certain aspects of a product ... the material and its source, for instance, as in the range of Bambu products produced for Artek, where the possibility of using an abundant and fast-growing plant with superior technical

qualities in a new way would have been a true inspiration to any designer. This project can challenge the use of finite raw materials and make an attempt at underdesign, where fashionability is engineered out of the product to give it a longer life, but might struggle to justify itself in a discussion about global distribution and a reduction in consumerism.

Clearly the only truly sustainable action might be to stop consuming at all, and perhaps we could add to that, stop making things as well, and perhaps even not breeding would really help a lot. A project aimed at exploring this possibility was 2nd Cycle, also for Artek, where a system of buying back Artek's old production was devised, and these chairs were put back into the sales channel, where they appealed to a new clientele, precisely because of their intrinsic uniqueness and patina gained over the years. All things considered, though, one can't help feel that a more active stance might be more appropriate, and surely for designers, inventors, manufacturers, and their customers, there are glints of positive practice emerging.

In this book, Marcus Fairs shines a light on a broad variety of projects, which in their diversity show some of the breadth of innovation that is currently active in this most important of sectors … giving us a tiny glimmer of hope in what can be a hugely depressing landscape, and shows us again that human ingenuity is the only way forward.

Tom Dixon

Below, left to right: 2nd Cycle, Eco Ware, Blow light, 2nd Cycle, all by Tom Dixon.

Introduction

In the last few years, green design has moved from being a fringe subject to being one of the most important areas of discussion in the design world. As concern about human-induced environmental degradation has risen to the top of the agenda, so designers have started to look seriously at their own activities and ask themselves whether they are part of the problem or part of the solution. Across the entire design spectrum, from architecture to car design to furniture and lighting, professionals are starting to address a different set of problems related not to the way things look and function but to their environmental and social impact. All of a sudden, it seems, energy-saving devices and gray-water recycling systems are de rigueur on architectural projects; car manufacturers are vying to produce vehicles with the lowest emissions; furniture and lighting made of recycled materials are at the height of fashion.

Long-established architects, including Richard Rogers and Norman Foster and designers such as Tom Dixon and Ross Lovegrove, are leading the charge, using their influence to convince clients that making their businesses, buildings, and products more sustainable is essential both morally and financially. At the same time, a new generation of young designers is emerging, reacting against the wastefulness of our consumer culture and instead exploring ways of creating new forms of design that are in harmony with nature, that do not consume irreplaceable resources, and that even challenge the notion of consumption itself.

Designers like Heath Nash, Tomás Gabzdil Libertiny, and Stuart Haygarth have become reluctant standard-bearers for a new set of green-oriented attitudes, partly as a result of attention from a voracious media eager to discover new trends—and there is no trend more marketable today than "green design." In the last couple of years there has also been a surge of books (such as this one), exhibitions, Web sites, blogs, and stores dedicated to green design, confirming that sustainability has gone mainstream.

This does not mean that we are witnessing a sudden avalanche of intelligent responses, revolutionary products, or even a consensus on what green design is. There is a lot of bandwagon-jumping, a lot of gimmickry, and a lot of far-fetched proposals that may never work or be of any benefit. But these are early days in design's green revolution: ideas are still being tested; technologies are still being perfected. Having been guilty in the past of paying too little attention to the environmental impact of what they do, designers are in many ways playing catch-up with rapidly changing attitudes to the environment. In architecture, for example, photovoltaics offer the promise that buildings could one day generate their own electricity from the power of the sun; but the solar cells first need to become much cheaper and much more efficient. In lighting design, new low-energy LED and CFL technologies are hampered by poor light quality and (in the case of CFLs) concerns over the safe disposal of expended bulbs. In automotive design, uncertainty over whether biofuels, hydrogen, or electricity will power the cars of the future—and concerns that consumers are not ready for such innovations—means manufacturers are experimenting cautiously.

It will take a major sea-change in consumer attitudes to—and in particular, the economics of—green technologies before they become mainstream. However, with oil prices in flux, concerns over fossil fuel supplies, and governments finally waking up to the threat of global warming, many experts believe the tipping point at which green alternatives become viable may be within reach.

The purpose of this book is not to present a manifesto, to moralize, or to establish criteria for what constitutes valid green design, but rather to present a snapshot of this surge in activity and to explain the forces and thought processes that are behind designers' work. The diverse range of projects shown here represents the disparate ways in which they are addressing green issues.

Green design can loosely be defined in terms of a set of objectives: to reduce the use of nonrenewable resources, both in the manufacturing process and in the finished object or building itself; to enhance the lives not just of users but also of everyone in the supply chain; and to minimize the environmental impact of the product or building during and after its useful life. This book focuses on designs that address one or more of these aims, encompassing projects that are environmentally or socially sustainable, or both.

The works selected for this book can be broadly divided into two camps: some are high-tech in their approach, and others low-tech. The former display a faith that technology can be harnessed to help solve environmental problems and is manifested in, for example, car designers' experimentations with innovations such as fuel-cell technology, hybrid engines, and regenerative braking. The low-tech approach, particularly prevalent among younger designers, involves eschewing technology in favor of rehabilitating long-established (and often ancient) processes, recycling waste materials, or mimicking natural systems. The fashion for repurposing used materials to create furniture, lighting, and homeware is one of the key design trends of our time, while projects such as Local River by Mathieu Lehanneur (see page 140)—a proposal for a futuristic domestic fish farm and vegetable propagator that promises healthier, more sustainable food—is based on agricultural techniques that have been in existence for hundreds of years. This low-tech tendency marks a striking departure from the accepted way designers have worked since the early twentieth century and suggests that young designers may be disillusioned with the status quo; they may even feel the design professions must collectively shoulder some responsibility for the situation we are in today. For most of the last century, designers were, by and large, uncritically committed to helping industry produce more and better goods for consumers, or producing buildings with more concern for economic parameters than their impact on people and the environment.

This complicity has helped propel us to our contemporary quandary. Climate change caused by carbon dioxide emissions from factories, buildings, and vehicles has emerged as the greatest threat to life on our planet, while the relentless scramble for resources to feed humanity's craving for consumer goods is a major cause of deforestation, pollution, and habitat destruction. Alongside is the human suffering caused by climate change–induced drought, conflict over resources, workplace exploitation, and lack of access to basic amenities, including clean water, health care, and education. Besides the environmental impact of our addiction to consumption, there is a substantial humanitarian cost borne most often by those who were the most disadvantaged in the first place.

The realization that consumer activities such as driving cars, flying in airplanes, heating homes, and using electrical appliances are causing direct damage to the planet seems to be causing designers—who are by and large an idealistic and conscientious bunch—to experience a sense of collective remorse that the products they bring into existence are often making things worse for society rather than better. The dream of the early-twentieth-century Modernists—that architects and designers could improve the lives of the masses through better-quality mass-produced goods—has turned out to be a chimera.

Yet designers are people who find solutions, and they are now turning their attention to the biggest problems of our age. While the idea that design might help to solve issues such as global warming and resource depletion is born of the unique circumstances of our time, green design today has clear parallels with earlier movements and thinkers who faced very different challenges. The Arts and Crafts movement at the end of the nineteenth century is often cited as an important precursor, since its adherents were spurred by a dislike of the way industrialization threatened to destroy the integrity of both the workers who labored in the factories and the objects they churned out. Instead, the movement promoted the dignity of skilled human labor, the honest use of materials, and the authenticity of form. The movement was both romantic—idealizing a mythical preindustrial era when skilled craftsmen worked natural materials to produce objects that were made to be used locally and to last—and elitist—the products and architecture it espoused were only affordable to a fortunate few. Nonetheless, it established a credible intellectual precedent for subsequent resistance to what would become the global consumerist economy.

The Arts and Crafts movement was ultimately supplanted by Modernism, which, rather than resisting technology, proposed to embrace and harness it for the good of all society. The intellectual focus moved away from the morality of production to the morality of consumption—people could gain dignity not through their labor but through their homes and possessions. Modernism was so successful that it became subsumed into materialism and became the official style of global corporatism, losing much of its radical social purpose in the process.

The author and educator Victor Papanek brought the notion that designers had moral obligations to society back onto the agenda with his influential 1971 book, *Design for the Real World*. Disaffected by the mismatch between design's power to shape our environment and the lack of any apparent concern from designers about the way their work was used to materialistic and trivial ends, Papanek set out a vision of design as an agent of positive change, with designers' skills harnessed to improve conditions in the developing world. William McDonough and Michael Braungart have proposed a still more radical approach to design and manufacture in their 2002 book *Cradle to Cradle*, subtitled "Remaking the Way We Make Things." This calls for an overhaul of the traditional manufacturing model, arguing that the three R's promoted by environmentalists—reduce, reuse, recycle—are all attempts to limit the exploitation of finite resources; instead, designers should be striving to eliminate the concept of waste altogether. Rather than "cradle to grave" products, which render useful materials unrecoverable, they argue that designers should start to consider how products' components could be endlessly "upcycled" to create new products or provide environmental nutrients. This radical design paradigm suggests that design could indeed one day help cure the problems facing the world today.

Previous page: Vase Monte Azul by Atelier NL; Right: Accordion House by 24H.

Lighting

There is a low-energy revolution under way in the lighting industry. New technologies that consume a fraction of the electricity while dramatically reducing the amount of heat generated are set to become widespread in the coming years, as the cost and quality of the fittings falls. Traditional incandescent bulbs—a technology that remains virtually unchanged since the days of Thomas Edison—may soon be obsolete, their demise hastened by increasing pressure from governments on manufacturers to phase out this energy-wasting technology.

In their place come two rival low-energy lighting systems: light-emitting diodes (LEDs) and compact fluorescent lamps (CFLs). LEDs are tiny electronic devices that can emit different colors of light, can be combined in arrays to create infinitely variable light qualities, and are dimmable. Their disadvantages are their cost and the fact that they generate some heat. CFLs—fluorescent bulbs containing a mixture of inert gas, mercury vapor, and phosphor—use around 60 percent less energy than incandescents, generate little heat, and last longer, yet there are concerns over the chemicals they contain. Both technologies are improving rapidly, but many designers remain dissatisfied by the quality of light they produce and—particularly in the case of CFLs—their ugliness. Designers and consumers alike seem reluctant to abandon the warm, comforting tones of traditional bulbs for the cold, harsh new light sources.

Designers are, however, beginning to explore the potential of these new technologies: CFLs, for example, have heralded a wave of delicate, decorative shades made of fabric, paper, and other fragile materials that could not be used close to the intense

heat of traditional incandescent bulbs. Meanwhile, Nicolas Roope's Plumen bulbs (see page 21) aim to turn the CFL itself into an object of beauty by giving it a variety of sculptural forms.

The potential to combine low-energy lights with renewable energy sources is producing new product typologies such as portable solar lights that harvest sunlight during the day and emit light at night, or lights that are powered by the wind. With their Portable Light Project, Kennedy & Violich Architecture are pushing these combined technologies further to develop a product of immense potential humanitarian benefit. By weaving extra-bright LEDs and photovoltaic cells into the same piece of fabric, the project is exploring ways of creating highly portable "light blankets" that would allow remote communities without electrical power from the grid to read and study after dark.

Yet, like designers working in other fields, many of the lighting designers featured in this chapter are using their products to make statements about environmental issues, rather than making products that are environmentally friendly. Using found or salvaged materials is a common technique: Stuart Haygarth's Optical chandelier, for example, is made from lenses salvaged from unwanted eyeglasses, while Committee's Kebab lamp is assembled from objects collected at flea markets and junk shops.

Although these designers are often motivated by aesthetics rather than politics—using waste materials because they find them beautiful—they are nonetheless helping to promote the notion that the most environmentally friendly products are those that are used, and reused, for generations.

Come Rain, Come Shine

Date **2004**
Designer **Tord Boontje**

Come Rain, Come Shine is a product from the Design with Conscience range produced by American design brand Artecnica, which promotes social sustainability and fair trade. In common with other items in the range, the light is handmade by artisans in the developing world, in this case by women working in a crafts cooperative in Brazil.

Come Rain, Come Shine is designed by Tord Boontje, a Dutch designer who is now based in the south of France. Available in black, white, and multicolored versions, the spectacular light shade consists of frothy hand-crocheted cotton, organza, and silk, and fabric flowers over a spherical structure of steel wire. The shades are fabricated at Coopa-Roca, a women's cooperative in Rocinha, a huge *favela* (shantytown) in Rio de Janeiro, using traditional Brazilian craft techniques such as appliqué, crochet, knotwork, and patchwork. Coopa-Roca—its full name is the Rocinha Seamstress and Craftwork Co-operative Ltd.—is an organization that allows women to work from home, so they can continue to look after their children and carry out domestic duties.

Artecnica's Design with Conscience project began in 2002 when the California company's founders, Enrico Bressan and Tahmineh Javanbakht, decided to shift their product range toward more sustainable designs (see pages 46, 50, and 64 for other products from the range). They were inspired by the postgraduate course in humanitarian design and sustainable style that was launched in the same year at the influential Design Academy Eindhoven in the Netherlands. The course was established by Dutch designer Hella Jongerius, who has since contributed products to the Design with Conscience range.

Artecnica's expanding Design with Conscience range pairs Western designers with skilled workers in the developing world, mostly in Asia and South America, where the work keeps traditional skills alive and allows workers to profit directly from their labor.

Blow Pendant Light

Date **2007**

Designer **Tom Dixon**

Compact fluorescent lamps (CFLs) use just 40 percent of the energy of traditional incandescent lightbulbs, but they have often been derided both for their ugliness and the poor quality of light they emit. Yet with the European Union seemingly committed to phasing out old-style incandescents, and the heat-generating bulbs' wastefulness beginning to attract the ire of environmentalists, many designers are now attempting to make CFLs more acceptable to consumers.

Tom Dixon's Blow pendant light, launched in 2007, is the first by the designer that is specifically designed to accommodate low-energy bulbs: the reflective copper finish on the shade creates a directional stream of light that flows through the clear plastic base. Rather than adopt a futuristic form, Dixon has opted for nostalgia: the light—which Dixon claims is one of the first CFL-friendly fittings that can be used outdoors—is modeled on the familiar bulging form of incandescent bulbs, thereby hiding the ugly low-energy light source in something more reassuring.

Dixon launched Blow during the London Design Festival in September 2007, teaming up with low-energy bulb manufacturer Glowb and UK energy-saving body the Energy Saving Trust to create an installation highlighting the energy-saving potential of CFLs. The installation, in Trafalgar Square in the center of London, featured 500 Blow lights with all-translucent shades suspended from a scaffold. During the week, 1,000 Blow lights and 3,500 Glowb CFL bulbs were given away to the public as part of an awareness-raising publicity stunt.

At the time, the Energy Saving Trust announced that if all 3,500 free lights were used to replace traditional 60-watt incandescents, they would lead to a saving of 831 tons of carbon dioxide during their lifespan—the equivalent of filling 150 hot-air balloons or 4,300 double-decker buses.

Wind to Light

Date **2007**

Designer **Jason Bruges Studio**

Created to explore ways of harnessing wind power in cities, this temporary installation at the South Bank Centre in London featured several hundred wind-powered LED lights mounted on tall, flexible rods that swayed in the wind. Each of the LEDs was powered by a miniature wind turbine, allowing the installation to give the effect of a swarm of lights that swayed back and forth and varied in intensity as the wind gusted around at night. The result was an ever-changing, three-dimensional visualization of wind patterns on the riverside site.

Wind to Light was designed by Jason Bruges Studio, a London-based design company that creates interactive artworks and installations. The studio has worked on many projects that explore environmental issues and make use of renewable energy. Phosphor Field, a similar installation proposed for Poole in southwest England, will involve dozens of phosphorescent lights atop swaying rods on a windy coastal site, showing the untapped power of the sea breezes. Another project at Aberafan in Wales will see a series of wind turbines installed at intervals along the coast. Colored LED lights embedded in the turbine blades will create swirling patterns of light, acting as wind-powered beacons and way-finding markers.

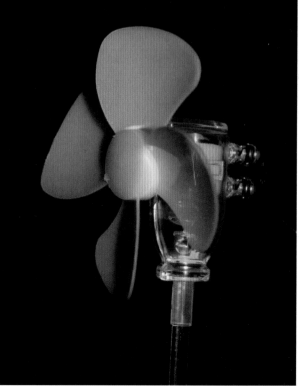

Litmus, completed in 2005 in Havering, London, involved four sculptural towers built on traffic circles. Each tower used a matrix of solar- or wind-powered LED lights to display details about the amount of power being generated, lighting levels, traffic volume, and the rise and fall of the tide on nearby marshes. The project aimed to give drivers, cocooned in their vehicles and thus cut off from their immediate environment, information about the natural world around them.

Optical Chandelier

Date **2007**
Designer **Stuart Haygarth**

Over three thousand glass lenses from unwanted prescription eyeglasses were used to create Optical, a spherical chandelier 5 feet (1.5 m) in diameter, with a single standard incandescent bulb at its center. The lenses are attached to nylon threads suspended from a ceiling-mounted grid.

Lighting designer Stuart Haygarth created the chandelier for Trash Luxe, an exhibition showcasing luxury design pieces made from unwanted or inexpensive materials, which was held at Liberty in London in September 2007. Many of Haygarth's pieces involve the painstaking assembly of found objects, seeking beauty in—and giving new life to—discarded items. Like fellow designers who work with found objects, Haygarth does not consider himself a "green" designer, yet his work often contains powerful narratives relating to the environment and contemporary values. Haygarth bought the lenses for Optical from a British charity that distributes discarded eyeglasses to the developing world, so the chandelier also serves as a reminder of global inequality in health care.

Similarly, Haygarth's Tide chandelier, first created in 2005, records the artificial debris washed up on Dungeness Beach in Kent, southeast England. For over two years, Haygarth collected and sorted objects discovered on the shore, reserving the small, translucent (and mainly plastic) items for his limited-edition chandeliers. Each Tide chandelier is 4 feet 7 inches (1.4 m) in diameter, contains roughly 1,100 objects—which include bottles, sunglasses, beach toys, and industrial components—and takes about a week to assemble, not including the time it takes to collect and wash the refuse. The objects are suspended in a spherical formation, which Haygarth says refers to the moon, which controls the ocean tides.

Other designs by Haygarth include the Disposable chandelier, a column 6 feet 7 inches (2 m) high, constructed of 416 disposable plastic wine glasses surrounding a pink fluorescent light source, and Shadey Family, a series of ceiling lights made from groups of mismatching, discarded glass lampshades.

Flame Lamps

Date **2007**
Designer **Gitta Gschwendtner**

Flame is another project that addresses the issues surrounding low-energy compact fluorescent lamps (CFLs). London-based designer Gitta Gschwendtner developed the project for 10 Again, an exhibition of sustainable products by ten designers that was held at the 100% Design trade show in London in September 2007.

Gschwendtner took as her starting point the perceived reluctance of consumers to switch to low-energy bulbs, which she felt was partly based on poor experiences they had had with an earlier generation of energy-saving bulbs that were promoted during the oil crisis of the 1970s. These bulbs were large, ugly, and produced a dim, flickering light.

The purpose of the Flame lamps project was to show that the latest CFL bulbs gave off a good quality of light and were attractive in their own right. Using a small candle-effect CFL bulb—designed to mimic the effect of a candle—Gschwendtner designed a series of ten lights, each of which referred to more traditional ways of generating light. Gschwendtner's lights featured bulbs set in candle wax, a pile of coal, a stack of wood, an oil canister, and a sheaf of paper. The idea was to show that using energy-saving bulbs could both help save nonrenewable energy sources while simultaneously giving light of comparable quality.

Plumen Low-Energy Bulbs

Date **2007**

Designer **Nicolas Roope**

Why are low-energy bulbs so ugly? That was the starting point for a design project initiated by Nicolas Roope of British technology brand Hulger, who felt that consumers would more readily switch to energy-saving products if they looked better.

Compact fluorescent lamps (CFLs) work in a similar way to fluorescent tube lights, with the long tube scaled down and folded or twisted so that it fits into a standard lamp holder. Whereas the globe-shaped form of the incandescent bulb is widely regarded as an icon of everyday design, the inelegant loops or swirls of CFLs have not endeared themselves to the public.

The Plumen project aims to make CFLs appealing in their own right, and not just items that are bought for moral reasons. The brand name Plumen is derived from a bird's plumage—the decorative feathers that have no practical purpose (that is, they do not aid flying)—and it also refers to the feather-like appearance of some of Roope's designs. Plumen concept designs—for which Roope is seeking

a manufacturer—also include sculptural knots, tubes flattened to look like ribbons, and balls that resemble diagrams of atoms.

CFL bulbs have recently become the subject of much debate, for although they offer energy savings of around 60 percent compared with incandescent bulbs and last much longer, there are concerns about the poor light quality they emit and the toxic chemicals they contain. CFLs contain a mixture of inert gas, mercury vapor, and phosphor. When an electric charge passes through the gas and mercury mixture, a plasma is created that produces ultraviolet light, which in turns causes the phosphor to fluoresce, producing light. Unless properly recycled, the poisonous mercury could leak in landfill sites, and the electrical circuitry contained in the bulb housing cannot easily be recycled. Despite this, many countries plan to phase out incandescent bulbs, with a voluntary agreement to come into force in the United Kingdom in 2009 (see also Tom Dixon's Blow pendant light, page 16).

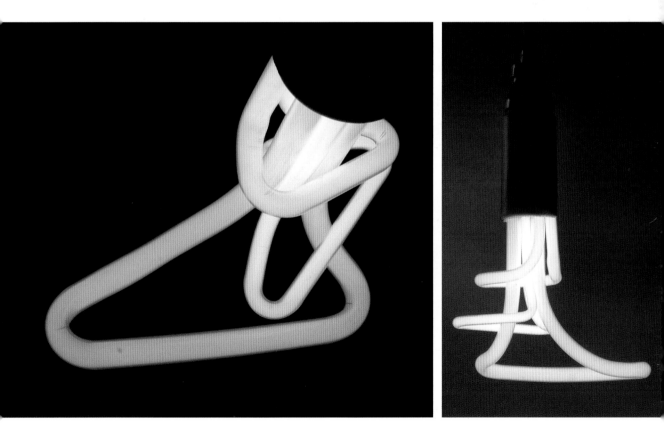

TransPlastic

Date **2007**

Designers **Humberto and Fernando Campana**

TransPlastic is the name of a large series of pieces developed in 2007 by leading Brazilian designers Humberto and Fernando Campana. The series consists of both lighting and furniture products that express the notion of nature claiming back the environment from people. This is achieved by working with two distinct materials: found plastic objects such as garden chairs and water containers, and a natural fiber called *apuí*. Relating a fantasy narrative developed by the brothers that has strong environmental undertones, the apuí feeds off the plastic, overpowering it and creating strange hybrid forms that are part natural and part artificial.

Apuí fibers come from a creeper, found in the Brazilian rain forests, which grows over trees, eventually suffocating and killing them. It is therefore a metaphor for the destruction that can be caused when one species becomes more powerful than others. Harvesting the fibers is thus a beneficial exercise, as it helps preserve biodiversity in the forests. Trees are not damaged by the harvesting, which is done by hand.

Using the fibers, the Campana brothers mimic what happens in the forests by weaving over and around plastic objects to create strange hybrid forms that partially swallow the host object.

There are two lighting products in the TransPlastic range: one that uses plastic water containers and another that uses white plastic balls. The water containers are stacked and linked by a structure of woven apuí, while the plastic balls become part of far larger and more organic pieces that the Campanas describe as meteors. These are large, undulating landscapes of apuí set with multiple plastic balls containing light sources. Some are designed to stand on the floor while others are intended to hang from the ceiling, where they resemble wicker clouds.

The range began when Humberto Campana started looking for a way to use the water containers he had been collecting for some time. The TransPlastic pieces are handmade in Brazil by artisans skilled in working with apuí.

Other People's Rubbish

Date **2006**

Designer **Heath Nash**

The tourist gift shops in Cape Town, South Africa, are filled with recycled souvenirs, including artifacts made from used aluminum drink cans and bottle tops. Other local craftsworkers weave vases and bowls from telephone wire or thin steel wire. These objects are often made in crafts cooperatives located in the vast shack districts that surround the city, where they provide much-needed employment. Many of these cooperatives are charities that support disabled workers or provide refuge for victims of domestic violence or AIDS sufferers.

Local artisans originally began using discarded trash or industrial offcuts as their raw materials because they were free and abundant, but as recycled objects have become fashionable due to their eco credentials, so this type of craftwork has begun to acquire status as objets d'art rather than mere tourist curios.

Cape Town designer Heath Nash has emerged as a leading figure on the local scene, taking the vernacular craft techniques and employing them to create lights and other objects, with a range he calls Other People's Rubbish. Nash often uses discarded plastic bottles, including white milk bottles and brightly colored containers from cleaning products, which he collects from recycling centers. He washes them thoroughly, then removes the top and bottom to create flat sheets, which he cuts and shapes to create floral lampshades. Nash stamps the flower and leaf shapes using a homemade cutter and a hammer, joining them together with wire. Nash also works with plastic bottle tops, which he joins together to create floor mats, and with woven wire, which he uses to make candelabra and other objects.

Unlike many of Cape Town's self-taught craftsworkers, Nash has an arts education, having studied sculpture at the University of Cape Town. He now employs five people and is developing an international reputation, exhibiting his work around the world.

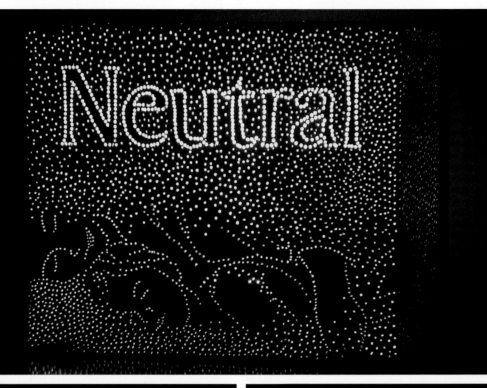

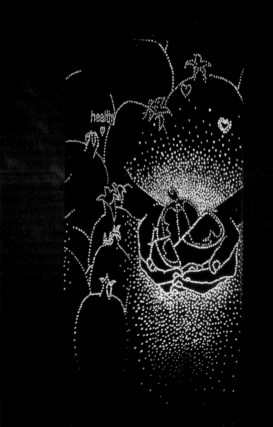

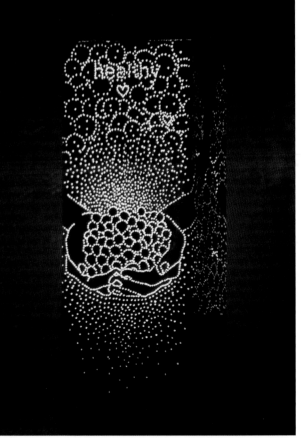

Packaging Lights

Date **2007**
Designer **Anke Weiss**

To create this series of lights, Dutch designer Anke Weiss took discarded laundry detergent containers, fruit-juice packs, cereal boxes, and so on and painstakingly traced elements of the images and text on their surfaces with a pin, making a matrix of tiny holes. She then placed a light source inside the packages, causing the pinprick patterns to glow as light floods through the holes.

This extremely simple idea is intended to show how unwanted objects can be turned into beautiful new products instead of being thrown away. Besides recycling the discarded packaging, the Packaging Lights project also cleverly turns the branding printed on the cardboard and plastic containers into strikingly beautiful new compositions. Rather than trace the brand's logo and imagery faithfully, Weiss only highlights certain elements of the package design to elicit unexpected compositions from otherwise familiar products. When the light sources are switched off, the packaging appears almost unaltered, but when switched on in a darkened room, the effect is magical and the product almost unrecognizable. As Weiss says, "The packaging exceeds its original context and gains the radiance of a shrine or icon."

The project has much in common with the work of other young designers, including Stuart Haygarth (see page 19), Harry Richardson and Clare Page of Committee (see page 30), and Heath Nash (see page 24), all of whom use discarded objects to create new pieces. Unlike these designers, however, Weiss leaves her salvaged objects pretty much intact, customizing them only with her pin rather than cutting and combining them with other objects.

Kebab Lamps

Date **2004**

Designers **Harry Richardson and Clare Page/Committee**

A subversive interpretation of a traditional standard lamp, Committee's Kebab lamps are among the earliest examples of what has now become a trend among designers for giving new life to abandoned objects. Each lamp consists of a vertical column of bric-a-brac drilled with a diamond-tipped bit, threaded onto a steel shaft, and topped with a colored shade.

Harry Richardson and Clare Page of London design team Committee devised the lamps partly as a joke but also as a deliberate reaction against the slick form-making of much contemporary design. Like many of their fellow designers, they do not see them as being concerned with recycling, although they have widely been interpreted as being part of the green design wave and have come to be regarded as icons of the new vogue for salvage-based design.

Rather than being random assemblies, each lamp is painstakingly and artfully composed of objects that tell a story or address a theme, and each one is given a distinct name. Poacher, for instance, is a reflection on the mythical English countryside and includes a ferret, an ornamental urn, a small silver hunting boot, and a plastic hedge trimmer (far left). Mountain Rescue, meanwhile, invites you to invent your own surreal, fairy tale–like narrative: a white ceramic stiletto is precariously balanced on a large plastic rock while an Eastern European peasant doll lies crushed between a cactus and a pink elephant (see left). The assemblage is capped with a small Hungarian china pot bearing a picture of a peasant girl dancing on top of a radio.

Richardson and Page scour junk shops and flea markets—notably the anarchic Deptford Market, a short walk from their London studio—for their incongruous materials, selecting worthless items such as single shoes or broken toys but also occasionally splashing out on pricier antiques that catch their eye.

Solar Bud

Date **1998**

Designer **Ross Lovegrove**

There are many solar-powered outdoor lights on the market, but Solar Bud was one of the very first and remains one of the most elegant. Designed by British designer Ross Lovegrove for Italian lighting brand Luceplan, and developed between 1995 and 1998, Solar Bud set the standard for such a product, consisting of a transparent mushroom-shaped light housing, which is set on a spike that is pushed into the ground.

The housing is made of molded, ultraviolet-resistant, clear polycarbonate, the parts of which are joined using ultrasonic welding to ensure they are waterproof. Inside, the housing contains an array of miniature photovoltaic cells and highly efficient LEDs. The spike is made of powder-coated aluminum tubing and contains a nickel-cadmium battery that stores the power harvested during the day to power the light during the night. A light detector automatically switches the product on in the evening.

Products such as Solar Bud give off a very limited amount of light and are more appropriate for providing decorative outdoor light, but they have the advantage of not requiring wiring or maintenance. Lovegrove has described the project as a statement of intent, designed to raise awareness of ecological considerations.

Solar Tree

Date **2007**
Designer **Ross Lovegrove**

The work of Welsh industrial designer Ross Lovegrove is characterized by organic forms inspired by natural processes such as the growth of plants, the flow of water, and DNA structures. In the sphere of lighting, Lovegrove has been exploring the potential of solar-powered products for many years, and attempting to integrate photovoltaic cells into products inspired by the forms of flowers, buds, and trees rather than simply bolting the panels onto existing products, as is the norm in the solar-lighting industry. His pioneering work in this field has already led to Solar Bud, a commercially available garden light (see page 31) and a conceptual solar-powered car (see pages 166–67).

Solar Tree is an ambitious attempt to develop a new typology for solar-powered street lighting. Created by Lovegrove in 2007 and temporarily installed in the street in front of the MAK museum of contemporary and applied arts in Vienna, the system is a speculative proposal intended to show how street lighting could be sculptural rather than simply utilitarian, as well being a net provider of power rather than a consumer.

The project was commissioned by MAK, who asked the designer to propose a design that would serve both an environmental and a social agenda. Working with Italian lighting brand Artemide and solar technology company Sharp Solar, Lovegrove developed a tree-like form of spreading steel branches, shaped using a new forming technique. Ten of the branches are topped with transparent pad-like forms that hold photovoltaic panels on their upper surfaces and contain light sources. Further branches are tipped with pinpoint light sources.

Besides being a beautifying structure, Solar Tree is intended to provide electrical charging points where pedestrians can recharge their mobile phones and laptops.

Sun Jar

Date **2006**

Designer **Tobias Wong**

Small solar-powered garden lights that charge during the day and emit light during the night are now cheap and easily available. They usually consist of glass lamps containing LEDs capped with a photovoltaic cell and mounted on a spike that is pushed into the ground (see Ross Lovegrove's Solar Bud, page 31).

American designer Tobias Wong has taken the technology used in these ubiquitous products and put them inside a standard Mason jar to create a very different, and far more poetic, product. Sun Jar is a domestic night light, designed to be used much as a candle or a lantern would have been used in the past. With the LED light source sealed inside a glass jar, it emits a warm orange glow that has about the same intensity as a candle. A second version comes with a blue light and is named Moon Jar.

Mason jars are glass containers with airtight lids and are used for culinary purposes such as fruit canning or pickling. Wong uses commercially available jars with flip-top lids and rubber seals. The seals are waterproof, meaning the light can also be used outside. The frosted glass surface diffuses the light.

The jar needs to be left in direct sunlight—either outside or on a sunny windowsill—during the day to charge the battery, which, when fully charged, gives around five hours of light. A daylight sensor automatically turns the light on when it gets dark, and there is a manual override switch that allows the user to turn the light off and conserve battery power.

Portable Light Project

Date **2005**

Designer **Kennedy & Violich Architecture**

Advances in lighting technology mean that tiny electronic light sources can be embedded in fabric, creating "sheets" of light. The latest flexible photovoltaic cells can similarly be attached to fabrics. Portable Light Project is an initiative exploring ways that these two technologies could be combined to help the estimated two billion people living in rural communities that do not have grid electricity.

The project began in 2005 at the University of Michigan's Nomads and Nanomaterials course—a course that brings together design, technology, and social action. Here, visiting professors Sheila Kennedy and Frano Violich of Kennedy & Violich Architecture asked students to look at ways to integrate high-brightness light-emitting diodes (HBLEDs) and photovoltaics into fabrics and clothing, so that users could harvest solar power by day to generate usable amounts of light to use at night.

For their research, the students and teachers visited the Huichol, a people descended from the Aztecs who live in rugged remote terrain in Mexico's Sierra Madre mountains. Here, the students developed a number of prototype products that integrated photovoltaics and HBLEDs into traditional Huichol objects, including knapsacks, mats, and canopies. Each object stores solar energy during the day, then at night the objects are reconfigured to serve as light sources.

Rather than sell these products to the Huichol, the idea was that they could buy the electronic components and weave them into fabrics themselves, using traditional techniques and materials, thereby ensuring the new objects were firmly rooted in local culture.

These prototypes were later refined into a concept for a reading mat that would allow Huichol children to study after dark. The mat can be rolled up for transportation and storage and can provide up to four hours' light for five hours' charging. The HBLEDs provide 160 lumens of light—enough for comfortable reading.

Portable Light Project was exhibited at the Design for the Other 90% exhibition at the Cooper-Hewitt Museum in Manhattan in 2007.

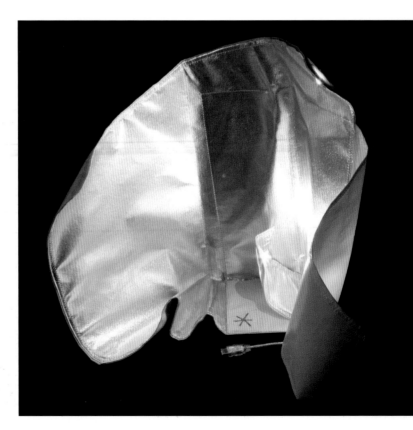

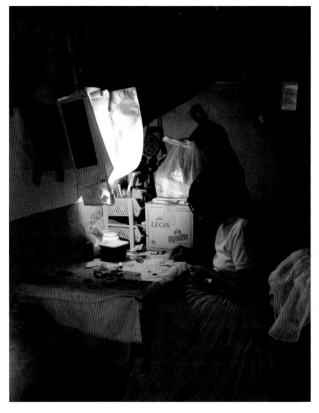

Daylight at Night

Date **2005**

Designer **Rebecca Potger**

The Daylight at Night lamp uses much the same technology as other solar-powered lights currently on the market, but it has a twist that makes its design unique. Based on the form of a traditional bedside lamp, the product is made of molded translucent polyethylene. LEDs are used as the light source, and solar power is harvested by a monocrystalline photovoltaic cell, with electricity stored in a lithium-ion battery. The lamp employs a technology called TSA Step-up Converter, which claims to boost the solar cells' power output by 300 percent compared with conventional cells. The lamp is waterproof and hence can be used outdoors as well as indoors. It gives up to forty hours' light from ten hours' charging outside in summer sunshine.

What makes the Daylight lamp unique is the fact that in order to charge it, it has to be turned upside down, since the solar cell is located on the base of the product. When inverted in this way, the lamp resembles a plant in a pot, making a visual metaphor for photosynthesis. When the lamp is required, it is turned upright again—an action that automatically switches the light on.

Daylight lamp was designed by Dutch designer Rebecca Potger while she was a student at Design Academy Eindhoven. It is now produced by her company, Potgerdesign.

Ninety

Date **2008**

Designer **Shawn Littrell**

Launched at the Stockholm Furniture Fair in 2008 by Norwegian lighting company Luxo, the Ninety claims to be the "world's most energy-efficient" task light. Consuming just 6 watts and designed to last twenty-five years, Ninety is one of several new lighting products that use light-emitting diodes (LEDs), small electronic semiconductors that emit light and consume even less energy than compact fluorescent lamps (CFLs). Unlike CFLs, they do not contain toxic chemicals. They are dimmable and can be made in a variety of colors, and can also be programmed to change the color of the light given off by varying the brightness of different-colored LEDs in an array.

The Ninety light, designed by American designer Shawn Littrell, uses just four LEDs, each consuming 1.5 watts and each surrounded by a reflector that, according to the manufacturers, doubles the amount of light falling on the work area compared with earlier LED lights. The low power consumption of the LEDs means the lamp head remains cool enough to touch even when the light is used at full brightness.

Lighting designers view LEDs as a technology that will revolutionize their sector, but there are a few hurdles to be overcome first. The main disadvantage of LEDs is their cost, but prices are already coming down sharply. A second disadvantage is that current LED technology tends to produce poor color rendering. Yet the lighting industry is confident that these issues will be addressed as technology improves. Since they are so small, LEDs can also be embedded in the surface of other objects, and designers, including Ingo Maurer, are experimenting with LED wallpaper. This type of application promises to revolutionize the possibilities of lighting design.

Light Bulb Packaging

Date **2007**

Designer **Olivia Cheung**

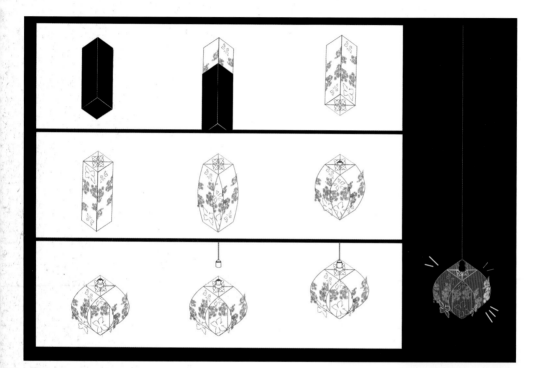

The amount of packaging required to protect a product during transportation and to make it alluring to the consumer is a subject of growing concern, especially as the packaging is usually thrown away as soon as the product is unwrapped. Designer Olivia Cheung has tackled this subject with Light Bulb Packaging, a conceptual product in which the packaging doubles as the shade for the light it contains.

The product consists of an energy-saving lightbulb contained within three boxes made of laser-cut vellum paper that nest inside each other, like Russian dolls. Each layer of paper—which is printed red on one side and left white on the other—is cut with a delicate floral pattern, but together the three layers of paper provide sufficient rigidity to protect the bulb.

The lightbulb's bayonet fixing protrudes from the packaging, and when this is inserted into a bulb holder, the packaging transmutes from a rectangular box into a spherical form to create a lampshade. The three layers of paper create a filigree screen around the bulb, as the floral cutouts become three-dimensional when the paper bends.

Cheung, who grew up in Canada, developed Light Bulb Packaging while studying 3D Design at the University of Brighton in England.

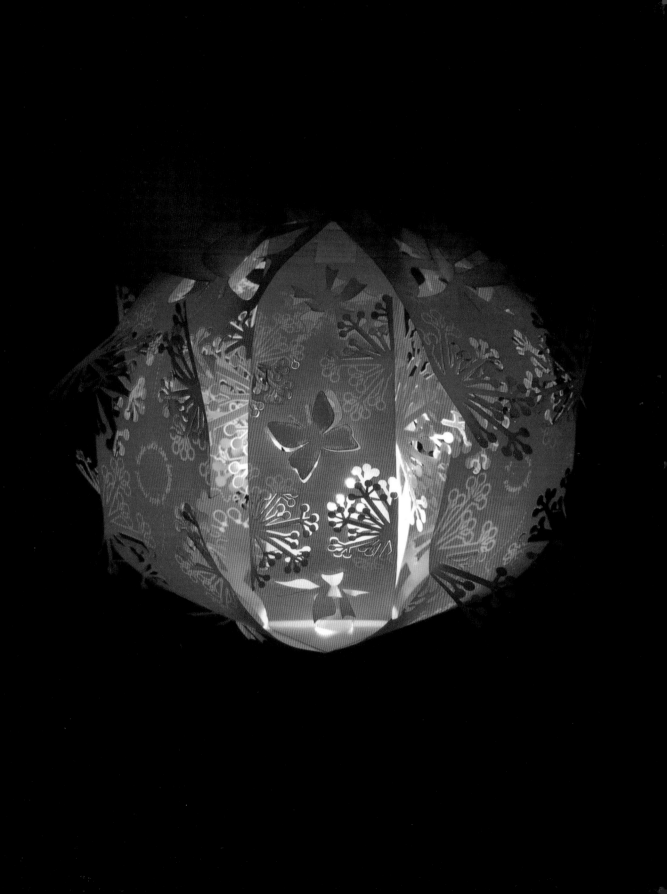

Light Wind

Date **2007**

Designer **Demakersvan**

Demakersvan, a team of young Dutch designers who met at Design Academy Eindhoven, turned to the windmills of their home country for the inspiration for this wind-powered outdoor lamp. The light is a curious hybrid of aesthetic references, with its propeller recalling early airplanes, its slender stem and shade resembling traditional domestic standard lamps, and its sail fabric covering suggesting sailing ships.

Called Light Wind, the product consists of a 7-foot 10-inch (2.4 m) standard lamp topped by a horizontally mounted propeller. The propeller, which is over 6 feet 6 inches (2 m) across, powers the lamp via a generator contained within the lamp housing. Both the wooden propeller and the lampshade are covered in sail fabric, reinforcing the connection with traditional windmills (Dutch mills featured canvas-covered sails).

Demakersvan's light is not yet in production and is a conceptual project as much as anything, designed to stimulate debate and explore new aesthetic possibilities for outdoor lighting products. But wind-powered lighting is already available commercially, although products on the market tend to lack the visual elegance of Demakersvan's design. Japanese electronics brand Panasonic produces a hybrid solar- and wind-powered street lighting system called Kaze Kamome. The lighting columns, topped with vertical-axis wind turbines and photovoltaic panels, were installed at the 2004 Olympics at Athens and at Expo 2005 at Aichi in Japan.

Hybrid systems such as this are also marketed by several other companies, while Hong Kong manufacturer Windsun Technology Enterprise Ltd. sells streetlights powered solely by the wind: the lighting columns feature propeller-type wind turbines that charge a battery during the day. Light sensors switch the streetlights on in the evening and off again in the morning. Without the need to be connected to a grid, such products allow street lighting to be installed in remote and developing areas of the world.

Homeware

The emergence of ethical business models in the design industry is one of the most interesting trends of recent years, as designers and manufacturers seek ways to help disadvantaged communities around the world while still producing profitable product lines. Mirroring the rise of the fair-trade movement, which aims to give small-scale food producers in the developing world a better deal, designers are starting to think carefully about the ethical implications of the way their products are manufactured.

Recent scandals regarding exploitation of workers in the clothing industry, for example, have focused consumers' attention on the fact that cheap goods bought in the West are often made by people in the developing world who are working in appalling conditions. This, combined with the revival of interest in handcrafted objects, has opened the door to companies such as American homeware brand Artecnica (see pages 46, 50, and 64) and Danish company Mater (page 58), both of whom see social sustainability as a vital part of their business.

Through its Design with a Conscience Range, Artecnica teams leading Western designers with artisan communities in the developing world who hand-produce the goods and receive a fair wage for their work. This pioneering initiative has now inspired other companies to do the same, with leading Italian furniture brand Cappellini launching a similar initiative called Cappellini Love in 2008.

Mater, meanwhile, works with factories in China, Vietnam, and India, but insists that suppliers sign up to rigorous environmental and social criteria to ensure that goods are produced with the minimum cost to both the environment and local communities. Thus globalization, which many see as a threat to local traditions and ways of life, is instead harnessed to match indigenous craft skills to the manufacture of niche products, with the designer acting as the go-between.

As with designers working in the areas of furniture and lighting, the use of recycled materials is a big theme in homeware today, with Christine Misiak lovingly restoring discarded tea sets and Atelier NL integrating discarded detergent bottles into new vases. The broad message here is that everything that once had a use can be put to new use, with the application of a little skill and imagination. Nothing need be thrown away.

Some of the most interesting products are the result of designers observing the resourcefulness of people from disadvantaged communities. Atelier NL's vases are the result of seeing how Brazilian shantytown dwellers use plastic bottles as vases, while Doshi Levien's Matlo watercooler is a direct interpretation of the highly efficient terra-cotta coolers that have been used in India for centuries. There is perhaps a growing realization that, in order to wean ourselves off our energy- and resource-intensive lifestyles, we in the West could do well to observe how those less fortunate than us live.

TranSglass

Date **1997**

Designers **Tord Boontje and Emma Woffenden**

Like many designers, Tord Boontje and Emma Woffenden started experimenting with waste objects early in their careers, as they could not afford to buy new materials. Boontje is a Dutch designer who set up a studio in London before he moved to the south of France with his partner, glass artist Emma Woffenden.

Boontje is now a very successful designer specializing in highly decorative lighting and products, but earlier in his career he explored the use of cheap, rough-edged materials to create low-tech, austere products. The TranSglass project came about when Boontje began to experiment with the glass-cutting tools in Woffenden's studio; he found he could transform discarded wine and beer bottles into vases and containers simply by making incisions with glass cutters and grinders. This simple technique created objects that are dramatically beautiful and not immediately recognizable as being made from mass-produced bottles, especially when the finished products are sandblasted to create a matte surface.

Boontje and Woffenden initially produced the TranSglass collection themselves, developing a wide range of objects. They later teamed up with American brand Artecnica, who now manufacture the TranSglass range as part of their Design with Conscience range (see also pages 14, 50, and 64), which pairs Western designers with artisans in the developing world in an attempt to keep indigenous skills alive while helping the craftsworkers develop high-value products that can be sold to global markets. As a result, the TranSglass range is now manufactured by craftsworkers in Guatemala. The project was set up with the help of Aid to Artisans, a charity that assists artisan communities around the world.

TranSglass has proven highly influential, and now several other designers are experimenting with techniques for transforming waste industrial glass into new, handcrafted objects.

Bush Glass

Date **2002**

Designers **Arnout Visser and Simon Barteling**

Kitengela is a glass studio near Nairobi in Kenya, set in grassland on the edge of the Nairobi National Park. Using a steam-powered glass oven under a large brick dome, the glass artists here—described as "the only Masai glassblowers in the world"—work with 100-percent recycled material made from broken window glass. The studio produces a variety of products, ranging from decorative objects to glass bricks, which they sell in an adjacent gallery.

Kitengela was founded in 1979 by German muralist Nani Croze as an artists community and "pioneer homestead" featuring a stained-glass studio. The glassblowing studio was added later by her son Anselm Croze, who now runs Kitengela, which also has studios for metalwork and other crafts. Kitengela's philosophy is heavily geared around recycling, with used oil firing the steam ovens and pulped-paper brickettes used as a construction material. Around 154 pounds (70 kg) of used window glass is melted down in the glass oven each day, producing a low-grade and unpredictable raw material that produces typically rough but characterful objects.

Dutch designers Arnout Visser and Simon Barteling have been visiting Kitengela for workshops since 2002, for what they call their Bush Glass project, collaborating with the resident glassblowers to experiment with new glassmaking techniques and creating a range of products. Besides the products created with recycled glass, the designers and glassblowers have also collaborated on products made from found glass objects such as cola bottles, which are blown into vases and lampshades, and eyeglass lenses, which they solder together to make lampshades. The lenses are taken from used eyeglasses that are shipped to Kenya from the West but which are not wanted in the country. The first workshops resulted in around fifty objects, which were exhibited at a gallery in Nairobi.

TransNeomatic

Date **2007**

Designers **Humberto and Fernando Campana**

Brazilian designers Fernando and Humberto Campana rose to international prominence around the turn of the twenty-first century through furniture designs based on the improvised creations of poor slum dwellers in their home town of São Paolo. Favela chair, their most famous piece, is an armchair made of hundreds of timber offcuts, resembling the ad hoc shantytown (*favela*) shelters constructed from scrap wood, while their Sushi chair is made from hundreds of strips of different kinds of fabric. Their work has been highly influential in terms of giving validity to a more chaotic, homemade design aesthetic, yet the Campanas' pieces were never really about recycling. Rather, they borrow the aesthetic of recycling: the Favela chair is in fact made of fresh-cut timber pieces, and the fabric for the Sushi chair is bought as new from fabric wholesalers.

However, with their TransNeomatic project, the brothers have attempted to address issues of both environmental and social sustainability. Commissioned as part of the Design with Conscience project initiated by American brand Artecnica (see also pages 14, 46, and 64), the brothers have designed a series of bowls featuring rims made from scooter tires salvaged from landfill dumps in Vietnam. The inner part of the bowls, meanwhile, are woven from wicker by Vietnamese artisans using traditional local techniques. Thus, the project aims to both reuse discarded materials and give work to skilled local craftsworkers.

When the design was first launched in 2007, there was suspicion over its authenticity, since the first samples—and those shown in publicity photos—appeared to be made from brand new tires. However, the brand and the designers moved quickly to point out that these were merely the prototypes produced in Brazil; the production versions, they promised, would indeed be made from recycled Vietnamese tires.

Green X-Mas Tree

Date **2007**

Designer **Büro North**

In 2007, Australian design company Büro North set out to design a product that was a greener alternative to those provided by the traditional Christmas tree industry, which has long been viewed as wasteful and destructive. Up to thirty-five million living fir trees are cut and transported for the Christmas market each year in the United States alone, according to the National Christmas Tree Association, with most of these ending up in landfill dumps—although the association also claims that each of the 500,000 acres under Christmas tree cultivation in the United States provides enough oxygen each day for eighteen people.

Büro North's solution was to create a reusable artificial tree made of plywood. Their design is manufactured from locally sourced plantation pine using CNC routing, a relatively low-energy production method; it comes flat-packed for more efficient transportation and storage during the rest of the year; and the design can be used again and again, unlike a real tree, which only gets used once.

The product, they claim, is "80 percent more environmentally friendly" than a real Christmas tree. They backed up their claims with a nine-page comparative life-cycle assessment (LCA), which compared their tree with traditional trees over five years. When taking into account the growth, transportation, retailing, maintenance, and disposal of five real trees over this period, the LCA calculated that the plywood tree generated less than 5 percent of the solid waste, used around a third of the water and embodied energy, and made one-fifth of the climate-change impact of a traditional tree.

Büro North also calculated the relatively tiny amount of carbon dioxide released during the manufacture and transportation of their tree over five years: the equivalent of growing 0.004 trees to maturity. The embodied energy used to produce the plywood tree is equal to a third of the daily power consumption of an average Australian household, the water consumed equals 0.7 of an average shower, and solid waste equates to 3 percent of a household garbage can.

The tree comes in three heights: 16 inches (40 cm), 37 inches (93 cm), and 91 inches (230 cm). However, with its high designer price tag, the product is significantly more expensive than a traditional Christmas tree.

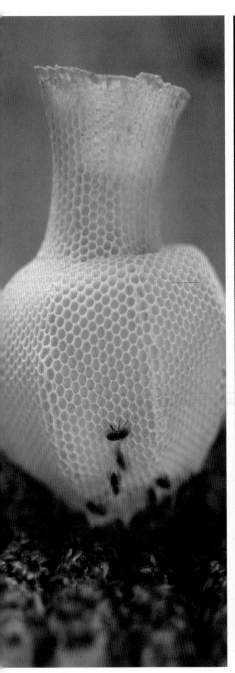

Honeycomb Vases

Date **2006**

Designer **Tomáš Gabzdil Libertiny**

Bee colonies have often been compared to factories, where worker bees collect raw materials in the form of pollen—used to feed larvae—and nectar, which is converted into honey, a food source for adult bees. Both honey and pollen are stored in hexagonal honeycomb cells—made from wax secreted by bees—until they are needed.

Slovakian-born designer Tomáš Gabzdil Libertiny of Studio Libertiny has harnessed the bees' honeycomb-forming activities to create a series of striking vases, called Honeycomb Vases. He effectively used a beehive as a factory to produce the objects. To make them, Libertiny first fabricated a prototypical vase shape from sheets of beeswax, the surface of which was embossed with a tessellated hexagon pattern. The vase was then placed inside a beehive and left for around a week. During this time, the bees in the colony built a honeycomb on the surface of the vase, using the embossed hexagonal pattern as a blueprint.

Libertiny calls the process "slow prototyping"—it took 40,000 bees one week to make each vase. Since bees become aggressive when they are interrupted, Libertiny had to guess when it was time to remove the vase. Each vase is totally unique, and Libertiny has experimented with hives in different regions, finding that each produces vases with a unique color and smell. Thus the vases are quite literally products of their environment, and since bees provide a vital service in pollinating plant species as they collect pollen and nectar, the fabrication of the vases could be argued to have had a beneficial effect on the environment. Honeycomb Vases are therefore a role model for "cradle to cradle" approaches to manufacturing.

Honeycomb Vases were first exhibited at the Milan Furniture Fair in April 2007 at a time when, unbeknownst to Libertiny, the American media was reporting the unexplained collapse of bee populations across the country. The vases therefore took on an additional, unintended cultural meaning, serving to remind observers of the miraculous but threatened creatures that created them.

Towel with Further Options

Date **2007**

Designers **Takuya Niimi and Yuki Niimi**

Many contemporary products have limited lifespans and are discarded and replaced when they start to show signs of wear. In the past, by contrast, shortages of materials or lack of money to buy new goods forced people to be more resourceful and find new uses for worn objects.

Towel with Further Options by Japanese designers Takuya Niimi and Yuki Niimi attempts to overcome contemporary wastefulness by creating a product that has a range of future uses built into it. The product begins as a large bath towel that has a grid-like pattern woven into the towelling. This pattern suggests ways that the towel can later be cut up into smaller pieces to become reappropriated first as a bath mat and then as a cleaning cloth as the nap of the fabric wears away. Cutting along these lines in the fabric means the new, smaller pieces of towelling will not fray, and look intentional rather than improvised.

The concept comes from the *yukata*—a casual form of kimono typically worn in Japan in the summer, and frequently worn after bathing at traditional Japanese inns. Like the more formal kimono, the yukata has straight seams and wide sleeves, but is usually made from cotton. Japanese people would traditionally cut up an old yukata to transform it into diapers or floor cloths, extending the useful life of the fabric once the garment had become old and worn. While this design is not radical, it serves to encourage people to cherish their possessions and to be inventive in order to avoid wasteful consumption—a "make do and mend" attitude that is seldom promoted by commercial products.

Towel with Further Options was awarded the Gold Prize by the judges of the 2007 MUJI Award, a prize given by the Japanese manufacturer to reward simple ideas for new products that would be easy to manufacture yet which show outstanding creative thought.

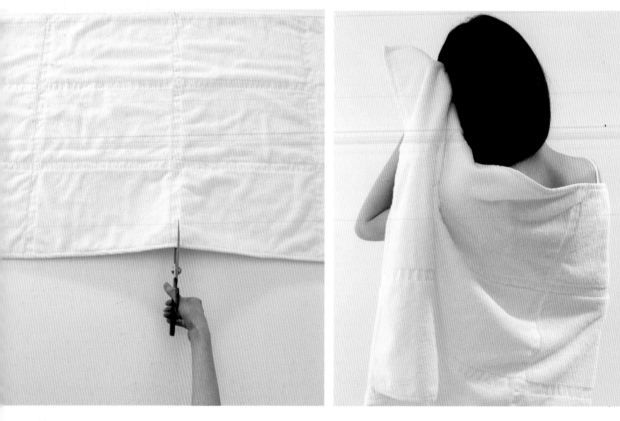

Tea Sets

Date **2007**

Designer **Christine Misiak**

This project by Polish designer Christine Misiak involves lovingly restoring discarded tea sets, and explores the changing relationship between consumers and objects in the United Kingdom, where she is now based. When metal tea sets were first used in Britain they were high status symbols, as tea was so expensive. Making tea was an important social ritual, and a broken teapot, sugar bowl, or milk jug would not be thrown away but carefully repaired. Yet changing social patterns and the advent of cheap mass-produced goods mean that nowadays teapots—like most other consumer goods—are discarded and replaced when broken.

Misiak began rescuing old, broken, and worn metal tea sets from garage sales and flea markets, and carefully restoring them as handcrafted objets d'art. She revives her finds with new components and surfaces painted in contemporary colors to make them into usable and desirable products once more. The sets are color-coded according to the process by which they have been rescued. For the green sets, Misiak removes the usable handles and feet from old items, cleans them up, and adds new metal bodies. The completed pieces are silver-plated, then selected parts are sprayed green. The orange sets signify that the teapot's handle was missing when Misiak found it, in which case she adds a new handle. The black sets are those where the surfaces were rusted, stained, or badly scratched. In these cases, Misiak polishes and powder-coats them to create a glossy, flawless surface.

Misiak's tea sets are thus a type of recycled product; however, like the work of many other contemporary designers who turn discarded objects into refurbished luxury goods, the true value of the pieces is to make people stop and think about today's throwaway culture.

I'm Not a Plastic Bag

Date **2007**

Designer **Anya Hindmarsh**

Plastic carrier bags have become one of the most conspicuous environmental scourges of our time. According to the social change movement We Are What We Do, each person uses an average of 167 plastic bags a year, and only one in every two hundred is recycled. The plastic can take up to four hundred years to break down in a landfill dump, and they are a major cause of death and injury to sea creatures such as turtles, which mistake them for jellyfish and eat them. They also cause flooding by clogging up drains in urban areas.

In 2007, British accessory designer Anya Hindmarsh teamed up with We Are What We Do to create a fashionable alternative to the plastic bag. The result was as much a marketing concept as a product: the organic unbleached cotton tote bag was printed with the prominent legend "I'm Not A Plastic Bag" and launched as a limited edition of twenty thousand in four colors.

The bags went on sale at Sainsbury's supermarkets in the United Kingdom in March 2007 for £5 each (nearly $10 in 2007, at a time when Hindmarsh's handbags usually sold for around £1,000). Massive media hype about the product ensured that thousands stood in line overnight for the bags, 100,000 people registered to buy them online, and they were soon changing hands on eBay for £200 each. Their cult status was assured when the bags were photographed on the arms of celebrities including actresses Keira Knightley and Reese Witherspoon and were given away at *Vanity Fair* magazine's Oscar night party.

The bag's phenomenal success was tempered by the discovery that the bags were manufactured in China and shipped to the West, leading to accusations that they were not as green as had been claimed. Nevertheless, the project did a huge amount to raise awareness of the environmental issues surrounding plastic bags, and proved that green consumption could be fashionable.

Mater Ethical Homeware Brand

Date **2007**

Designers **Various**

Launched in 2007, Mater is a homeware brand based in Copenhagen that is committed to sourcing socially sustainable products. Mater—Latin for "mother"—sells a range of products including lamps, bowls, vases, and candleholders, made from natural materials such as wood, stone, and ceramic as well as metals including steel, brass, and aluminum. The objects are designed by European and American designers that include Jens Martin Skibsted and Todd Bracher, and are manufactured in China, Vietnam, and India, largely by small and medium-sized companies that are subjected to rigorous vetting procedures to ensure they meet high standards of corporate social sustainability.

Mater also aims to foster, rather than threaten, indigenous craft skills. The Marble/Wood collection of candelabra by American designer Todd Bracher, for example, was developed in Jaipur, India, in collaboration with local artisans. The products use marble and timber that are unique to the region, but not rare.

Unusually, Mater publishes details of the companies that produce its goods as well as the names of the designers, giving equal billing to the usually faceless factories that turn out most designer goods. To avoid accusations that it is exploiting cheap Eastern labor, Mater operates a "zero tolerance" policy in regard to human rights in its suppliers' factories, and promises to terminate contracts with any company found to be using child labor, mistreating employees, or causing pollution. Mater has signed up to the United Nations Declaration of Human Rights, the United Nations Global Compact, and the International Labour Organization's Fundamental Principles and Rights at Work. To prove its commitment to fairness and transparency, the brand promises to commission independent audits of suppliers' factories and to publish the results on its Web site.

Mater's products are designed to last for a long time, hence their robust materials and their simple, typically Scandinavian forms that are intended to be timeless rather than fashionable.

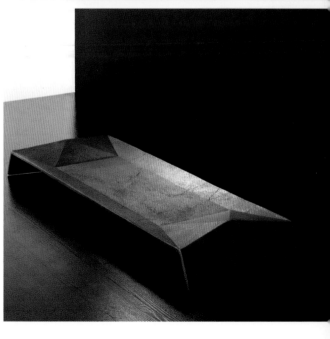

Pulp

Date **2007**

Designer **Jo Meesters**

This project is an exploration of the possibilities of using waste-paper pulp to produce resilient objects that can hold water. Created by Dutch designer Jo Meesters, the vases and jugs are created from pulp from shredded newspapers mixed with wallpaper glue and ink, and lined with epoxy resin to make them waterproof. The pulp is molded around discarded pots and vases found at flea markets, giving the products a smooth internal surface, although the external finish is somewhat primitive looking.

The process is akin to papier-mâché, but Meesters first dissolves the shredded paper in a mixture of boiling water and sodium carbonate to reduce it to a fine pulp. It is left to break down for two weeks before being mixed with the glue and ink and applied by hand to the mold, layer by layer, with each layer allowed to dry before the next is applied. Once the required thickness is achieved, the vase is cut in two vertically so that the mold can be retrieved and used again. The two halves of the vase are then joined back together using wood glue, and additional pulp is applied until the join cannot be seen and the vase is deemed strong enough. The final stage of the process is to apply polyurethane to the inner surface to render the object waterproof.

Pulp was not conceived with sustainability in mind, and the use of inks, glues, and polyurethane would lead green purists to reject the products on these grounds. But the project does show how waste materials such as newspaper have the potential to be transformed into entirely new materials that do not conform to the sometimes clichéd appearance of "recycled" objects.

Eco Ware

Date **2003**

Designer **Tom Dixon**

Contemporary consumer culture revolves around the notion of disposability—objects are used for a while and then thrown away, even when the objects are made of durable materials that could last for years. British designer Tom Dixon explores this issue with his Eco Ware range of cups, plates, and bowls, which are literally designed to wear away. The rugged, earthy-looking range, launched at the Milan Furniture Fair in 2003, is molded from an all-natural plastic consisting of 85 percent bamboo fiber—a by-product of the bamboo processing industry that would otherwise be thrown away.

Bamboo offcuts, salvaged from factories turning the wood into furniture and flooring, are ground to a powder and mixed with a water-soluble polymer to create a tough, durable thermosetting plastic material that resembles Bakelite and that can be molded like traditional plastics. Similar materials have been developed using other organic by-products such as coconut husks or rice fibers.

The drawback is that the material is biodegradable—it degrades over time as the products are used and washed, their shiny, smooth surfaces eroding away. But Dixon has turned this into an advantage, pointing out that the objects take on a new and more interesting character as they are used, becoming unique and personal to the user.

Their lifespan is around five years, which is similar to the expected life of many items of tableware made from more durable materials—and after this time they can be reused as plant pots or composted rather than thrown away. Eco Ware therefore represents one of the more successful attempts by designers to create genuinely sustainable products, although Dixon has admitted that there has been some consumer resistance to the notion of a designer product that has a limited lifespan.

As scientists develop better-performing organic-based plastics, domestic products with short lifespans may increasingly be produced from biodegradable materials.

Secondhand Plates and Unmade 07

Date **2006, 2007**

Designer **Karen Ryan**

Like many young designers, Karen Ryan prefers to work with found objects, reevaluating the beauty and value of things others have thrown away and putting them to new uses. Like fellow designers including Stuart Haygarth and the Campana brothers (see pages 19, 23, and 50), Ryan does not do this to promote a green message, but instead out of a fascination with the material qualities—and the emotional effects—of old or unwanted artificial objects.

The British designer's Unmade 07 collection of vases, created in 2007, is made from old porcelain vases that Ryan finds in secondhand shops and flea markets. First, part of the surface is masked off to form an "Unmade 07" logo, which protects the original surface beneath; then Ryan grinds off the glazed surfaces and applied decoration of her finds to reveal the raw ceramic beneath. Removing the mask leaves the logo standing proud, hinting at the decoration that once graced the vase while at the same time decisively rebranding the object as something new.

This project followed a similar series created in 2006 called Secondhand Plates. These are unwanted dinner plates and side plates, decorated with a willow pattern or kitsch rustic scenes, which Ryan bought in thrift stores or at garage sales. As with Unmade 07, Ryan masks off part of the surfaces before sandblasting them, this time creating words with negative connotations such as "neglect," "loss," "envy," and "vanity." Spelled out in the original surface decoration, this turns the original quaint design into something more disturbing.

An earlier project in this vein, which Ryan started in 2005, is her Custom Made furniture—secondhand chairs and tables that are painted with striking patterns of stripes in bright gloss, or combined with other pieces to create strange new forms.

Beads and Pieces

Date **2005**
Designer **Hella Jongerius**

Dutch designer Hella Jongerius often explores craft processes in her work and has collaborated with long-established manufacturers in her native Netherlands as well as in Japan and the United States. This collection of domestic objects was developed in collaboration with artisans in Peru and is inspired by the traditional ceramics and beadwork of the Shipibo people. The four objects—a vase and three bowls—employ the black ceramic typical of the ethnic group while the decorative beadwork is inspired by local motifs that celebrate the farming and processing of the coca plant—an industry of vital economic, as well as symbolic, importance to the region.

Jongerius designed the range for Artecnica's Design with Conscience project (see pages 14, 46, and 60), which pairs leading designers with craft communities in order to keep local skills alive; artisans in the Lima region of Peru produce the pieces for Artecnica. The range was developed in collaboration with the nonprofit body Aid to Artisans, an organization that helps traditional craftsworkers around the world develop better products and business skills. The range was launched at the International Contemporary Furniture Fair in New York City in 2005 and went into production the following year.

Matlo Water Holder

Date **2005**

Designers **Nipa Doshi and Jonathan Levien/Doshi Levien**

When water evaporates through the surface of a closed terra-cotta vessel, the tiny droplets take heat with them, which has the effect of cooling the water that remains in the vessel. The process is similar to the way that perspiration evaporating from human skin removes heat from the body, keeping it cool after exertion or in hot weather. Well known around the world for this simple and effective process, terra-cotta water holders have long been used for water storage in hot countries. Such containers can cool water to 22–25 degrees Fahrenheit (12–14 degrees Celsius) below the ambient temperature without the need for artificial refrigeration.

Matlo is a contemporary design for a water holder based on traditional principles, and created by Anglo-Indian designers Nipa Doshi and Jonathan Levien of London-based company Doshi Levien. The duo first designed the product for an exhibition sponsored by the British Council at the Experimenta Design 2005 Biennale in Lisbon, Portugal. Called "My World," the show explored how young designers were interpreting the notion of craft. Doshi Levien's installation at the "My World" exhibition was partly inspired by the traditional markets of India, where customers remove their shoes, sit on a mattress, and discuss their needs with the stallholder, who is often a skilled artisan who makes the goods on the premises.

The duo created a series of objects based on Indian archetypes for their installation, including a fan, a marble table, and the Matlo watercooler, which is a common feature in such shops in India. Their version is intended as a prototype for possible mass production or batch production, and features a slip-cast terra-cotta vessel containing a filtration system.

The product is intended as an environmentally sound alternative to bottled water and electric coolers, and a more elegant and culturally appropriate addition to the interior landscape.

Vase Monte Azul

Date **2006**

Designers **Lonny van Rijswijck and Nadine Sterk/Atelier NL**

Many designers admire the resourcefulness shown by people who do not have the means to buy the items they need and instead improvise by putting broken or discarded objects to new purposes.

While on a field trip to Brazil when studying at Design Academy Eindhoven in the Netherlands, young Dutch designers Lonny van Rijswijck and Nadine Sterk, who now work under the studio name Atelier NL, noticed the way inhabitants in the slums used discarded plastic detergent bottles as flower vases.

Van Rijswijck and Sterk had traveled to Brazil as part of a social project aimed at helping poor communities develop new business opportunities, and they decided to use this observation as the basis for a product that could be made and sold by the local community.

Vase Monte Azul is named after the *favela* (shantytown) of Monte Azul on the outskirts of São Paolo. The vase has at its core a plastic bottle scavenged by collectors from the slum. The bottle is contained within a turned wooden body that is capable of being made on a simple lathe. The plastic and the wood are an unlikely combination for a vase, but they work well together, since the bottle serves as a waterproof core that stops the wood from getting wet and decaying.

On returning home from Brazil, the designers showed the vase to the influential Dutch design brand Droog, who included it in their collection and held an auction to raise money for a semiautomatic lathe—this allows the inhabitants of Monte Azul to continue to produce the vase themselves.

Drawn from Clay (Uit die Klei Getrokken)

Date **2006**

Designer **Lonny van Rijswijck/Atelier NL**

Globalization means that people in different parts of the world often use identical products, since economies of scale often make it cheaper to buy mass-produced imported items rather than locally manufactured ones. This leads to fears of a loss of cultural identity, and raises concerns about the wastefulness of shipping items across long distances when they could be fabricated closer to the places where they will be used.

Lonny van Rijswijck of Dutch design firm Atelier NL is among several designers who are exploring these issues and creating products that are made from natural materials specific to the places they are produced.

Her Drawn from Clay (*Uit de Klei Getrokken*) project is a range of cups and saucers made from clay dug up from a variety of locations in the Netherlands. The town of Brunssum in the southeast Netherlands yields a yellow clay that appears frosted when glazed; Woerden in the center of the country produces a smooth, shiny, dark-brown clay; and Gilze-Rijen in the south produces a rough terra-cotta.

The subtle differences in the color and texture of each clay highlights the rich variety of materials that are available to designers but which are often ignored in favor of a few standard materials, and shows how objects made with indigenous materials can be more culturally meaningful as well as more sustainable.

Furniture

Furniture designers are suddenly at the vanguard of green design thinking. A new wave of young, independent designers is creating everyday items such as tables, chairs, and cupboards that double as manifestos for a new, less-wasteful way of living.

The creative reuse of existing materials is central to this new movement, with figures such as Martino Gamper, Maarten Baas, Christian Kocx, and Ryan Frank taking waste wood, factory offcuts, and salvaged junk to make new items. Their motives are often not environmental per se, but are instead driven by an appreciation for the often overlooked beauty that can be found in things other people throw away.

This movement is also a reaction against the way that furniture design—assisted by a powerful media that constantly requires new products to publish—has become akin to the fashion industry in recent years, with interior style trends changing every season and consumers encouraged to replace items regularly to keep up. Yet items of furniture used to be considered heirlooms, to be looked after and handed down through the generations. New designers are rediscovering this attitude with their often unique, handmade creations, designed to last years.

Finnish brand Artek, under the creative direction of designer Tom Dixon, is pursuing a similar philosophy with the 2nd Cycle range. This project involves tracking down vintage Artek items—which have often been repainted, reupholstered, or otherwise customized by a series of owners—and recording

their unique histories. The message here is that a fifty-year-old stool that looks battered and worn is in fact a living piece of history and, as such, is more valuable than a new one. Dixon is also encouraging Artek to explore more sustainable raw materials such as bamboo, while TAF Arkitektkontor's IOU Design for Charity range not only uses renewable timber but also benefits less fortunate members of society, who are employed to assemble the pieces.

Not all designs made from recycled materials need adopt the fashionable "salvaged" look. Nendo's Cabbage chair is made from wastepaper that is a by-product of the fabric pleating industry, yet its sophisticated look belies the unwanted raw material from which it is made.

Other designers sourcing greener materials include Norman Foster, whose 20-06 chair for Emeco is made from 80 percent recycled aluminum, and Komplot, whose Nobody chair is made from recycled PET water bottles. With their Pano chair, French designers Studio Lo have created a flat-pack item that uses plywood sheet as efficiently as possible to minimize waste.

Given that well-designed furniture should last a lifetime, all these designers are trying to produce objects that exist outside the fickle world of interior trends and instead embody distinctly unfashionable qualities such as solidity, longevity, and the ability to wear the damage accrued over the years, not as imperfections but as signs of character.

Cabbage Chair

Date **2008**

Designer **Nendo**

In the early 1990s, fashion designer Issey Miyake introduced a fashion line called Pleats Please—a range of clothes made from fabric that is pleated after the garment has been sewn. To make the pleats stay in place, the garments are sandwiched between layers of fine paper and placed in a heat press. After the heat has "sealed" the pleats into the fabric, the paper is then discarded.

In 2008, Mikaye asked Japanese design team Nendo to develop a product using this unwanted paper. Nendo's response was the Cabbage chair, a simple design that can be made entirely by hand without specialized tools or materials.

To create the chair, the paper is wrapped into a cylinder. The cylinder is then cut vertically from the top down to the midpoint. Then the individual layers of paper are peeled and folded one at a time, creating both the form of the chair and sufficient structural rigidity to allow someone to sit in the chair. The name derives from its similarity to the way the individually flimsy leaves of a cabbage are built up in layers to create a robust whole.

Nendo designed the chair for XXIst Century Man, an exhibition curated by Miyake, at 21_21 Design Sight in Tokyo from March to July 2008. 21_21 Design Sight is a cultural foundation set up by Miyake in Roppongi, and the XXIst Century Man exhibition explored how designers were responding to contemporary concerns, including environmental issues.

TaTu

Date **2006**

Designer **Stephen Burks**

Items fabricated from galvanized steel wire are common in South Africa, where artisans turn this cheap, readily available material into small domestic objects such as bowls, as well as curios for tourists. The technique involves manipulating coils of thick wire to form a three-dimensional form, which is then given strength by attaching crosspieces with thinner wire.

Stephen Burks, an industrial designer who runs a New York City design studio called Readymade Projects, came across the technique while in South Africa as part of design brand Artecnica's Design with Conscience project—an initiative that pairs Western designers with artisans in the developing world (see pages 14, 46, 50, and 64).

Burks began speaking to an artisan working with the material and asked him if it was possible to use the technique to make a larger object. The result of the conversation was a new design for a collection of modular side and coffee tables that are composed of three separate hollow elements, which can be used for storage. A one-piece stool is also part of the collection.

The collection is called TaTu, which means "three" in the Shona language, in reference to the way that the table is made of three separate parts—the stand, top, and lid—which, when taken apart, can be used respectively as baskets, bowls, and trays. The pieces are made using the same traditional wire-working technique and are fabricated in Africa by South African and Zimbabwean artisans for Artecnica. The pieces are finished in red or white polished powder coating to make them suitable for indoor or outdoor use.

Scrapwood Furniture

Date **2005**
Designer **Piet Hein Eek**

Dutch designer Piet Hein Eek is one of the pioneers of the recent design movement that creates luxurious products from cheap or unwanted source materials. In Eek's case, as with many of his fellow designers, this is not so much due to a concern for environmental issues but rather an appreciation of the beauty of materials—particularly scrap timber—that would otherwise be considered waste.

Eek works in a variety of materials including steel, aluminum, ceramic, and polycarbonate, and is a prolific designer of furniture, lighting, and other products. But he is best known for his Scrapwood series of chairs, tables, and sideboards made from salvaged wood. A graduate of the Design Academy Eindhoven in 1990, he first came to prominence when one of his recycled chests of drawers was exhibited in Milan by the then-fledgling brand Droog. In common with other young Dutch designers at the time, Eek was bored with conventional notions of beauty and the sleek perfection of most contemporary furniture design. He started to use wooden floorboards and planks salvaged from demolished or abandoned buildings, treating the worthless materials as if they were precious and lovingly crafting them into new pieces. Often Eek leaves the wood's original finish intact, with pieces such as those shown here displaying a multitude of different paint and varnish finishes that survive from their original uses.

Based in Geldrop in the Netherlands, Eek has recently experienced something of a revival in popularity as recycling and customization return to fashion and consumers start to shun anonymous mass-produced items for those that have character and personality. In 2005 he exhibited in London and Tokyo, and his pieces—which are renowned for their exquisite carpentry—have started to become highly collectable, selling through art galleries.

20-06 Chair

Date **2006**

Designer **Norman Foster**

Aluminum is the third most abundant element on earth, after oxygen and silicon, and the metal is highly resistant to corrosion and extremely lightweight. The smelting of aluminum ore to extract aluminum requires vasts amounts of electricity, but once the metal has been processed it can be reused again and again. Melting down and recycling aluminum requires only 5 percent of the energy used to extract the metal in the first place, although around 15 percent of the metal is lost during the process, turning to an unusable ash-like oxide.

This stackable chair, designed by British architect Norman Foster for the Pennsylvania furniture manufacturer Emeco, is made of 80 percent recycled aluminum, half of which is from used drink cans while the other half comes from industrial scrap. The chair has been engineered to use as little of the material as possible, although this is done more for aesthetic than ecological reasons. But the chair has an estimated lifespan of 150 years, making it a highly sustainable design.

Emeco—the Electric Machine and Equipment Company—has been handmaking aluminum chairs and stools since 1944, when it created the iconic 10-06 chair for the U.S. submarine fleet with the collaboration of Alcoa, the world's third-largest producer of aluminum. Better known as the Navy chair, it has been in continuous production ever since and, like Foster's chair, is designed to last 150 years. Foster's 20-06 chair, launched in 2006, updates the original design but uses 15 percent less aluminum. Like its predecessor, it can be stacked up to ten chairs high and has now been expanded into a product range that includes bar stools and café tables.

Emeco's products are made using a laborious 77-stage process of welding and grinding, carried out by highly skilled craftsmen. Emeco has also developed aluminum chairs with other leading designers, including Philippe Starck (Icon, Kong, Heritage, and Hudson), Frank Gehry (Superlight), and Ettore Sottsass (Nine-O).

Bambu Furniture

Date **2006**

Designer **Henrik Tjaerby**

Bamboo is one of the most versatile renewable materials. These woody, evergreen perennials are the largest members of the grass family, are easy to cultivate, and grow extremely quickly—up to 3 feet (1 m) a day—and their timber is lightweight, durable, and strong and does not shrink and expand as much as other woods.

Long used in the Far East for making everything from chopsticks to houses, bamboo is increasingly being used in the West to make furniture, flooring, and even car interiors. The wood is also increasingly being processed to create laminates, plywood, and natural plastics, such as for Tom Dixon's Eco Ware cups and plates (see page 61).

Danish designer Henrik Tjaerby launched his Bambu range of furniture in 2006 in collaboration with the in-house design studio at Finnish furniture brand Artek. Consisting of a chair, dining table, and coffee table, the range is made of laminated bamboo strips that are harvested in China and manufactured in Japan.

With a nod to Artek's Scandinavian heritage (see page 84), the bamboo is steam-bent into shape, employing a similar technique to that used to make the bent birch-ply furniture designed for the brand in the 1930s by the influential Finnish architect Alvar Aalto, who was one of Artek's cofounders.

In fact, Tjaerby has compared bamboo to Scandinavian birch: both are humble materials that are abundant and fast-growing, and both are relatively undervalued in their native markets. Bambu is an attempt to demonstrate that bamboo can be used to create furniture that is stylish and contemporary as well as green.

The Bambu range was the brainchild of British designer Tom Dixon, who became Artek's creative director in 2005 and is now helping the brand become a leader in sustainable design. Other initiatives Dixon has launched for the brand include the 2nd Cycle project and the Artek Pavilion (see pages 84 and 231).

Nobody Chair

Date **2007**

Designers **Boris Berlin and Poul Christiansen/Komplot**

The Nobody chair by Boris Berlin and Poul Christiansen of Danish design company Komplot is made from recycled plastic water bottles using a manufacturing technique borrowed from the car industry. Produced for Danish furniture brand Hay, the chair is pressed in a single piece from industrial felt made of recovered polyethylene terephthalate (PET), employing the same process used to form the removable shelves in car trunks. Hay claims it is the first chair ever to be mass-produced using nothing but textiles—the chair does not have a frame or contain any additional reinforcements, fixtures, or glue (hence the name "no body" chair). Instead, it relies solely on the structural integrity of the pressed felt. The product is made in a single step: felt made from PET fibers is placed inside a large press and heated up until it permanently takes on the chair shape.

Polyethylene terephthalate (PET) is a type of polyester and is commonly used to make synthetic fibers as well as bottles.

The felt used to make the Nobody chair comes mainly from PET recovered from used plastic water bottles. This is one of the most common sources of recycled plastics, since most brands of drinking water use exactly the same type of plastic, meaning it is relatively easy to sort the material for recovery. Other types of plastic containers, for example shampoo bottles, are made from many different kinds of plastic and are therefore almost impossible to recycle without mixing different types of plastic, which results in material that is of a lower grade and therefore less useful. The pure PET in the Nobody chair, however, can potentially be recycled again in future.

Besides its environmental credentials, the Nobody chair's designers claim it has other benefits. It is stackable, making it a space-saving design, while the PET felt's textile-like quality means the chair gives the sitter the feeling that it is covered in fabric.

2nd Cycle

Date **2007**

Designers **Tom Dixon/Artek**

Finnish furniture brand Artek was founded in 1935 along Modernist principles by a group of designers led by the architect Alvar Aalto. Several of Aalto's designs—including pared-down chairs, stools, and tables made of steam-bent birch ply—have been in continuous production ever since, and many early Artek items are still in use today in homes, public buildings, and schools in Finland. These vintage pieces are often worn and shabby-looking, and many have been customized by their owners with paint or upholstery, but their solid construction means they are still perfectly functional, and the patina of age gives these mass-produced pieces individual personalities.

A piece of furniture that has been in use for over seventy years is clearly a highly sustainable piece of design—especially if it was made of natural materials in the first place. As part of its environmental strategy, Artek has decided to draw attention to the longevity of its products. The 2nd Cycle project involves finding early Artek furniture, buying the pieces back from their owners, and researching the individual history of each piece.

Once the unique history of an item has been compiled, it is uploaded to a Web site. The item of furniture is left exactly as it was found—it is not restored in any way—save for the addition of a radio-frequency identification (RFID) tag, which is embedded in the item. The tag can be read by a mobile phone, revealing the Web address, so new owners can then look up the item's history on the Internet. Once the furniture has been catalogued, it is put back into circulation either by being sold or used at events, and future users are encouraged to add their own stories to the object's accumulated history.

2nd Cycle was initiated in 2007 by designer Tom Dixon, who is Artek's creative director, as a way of initiating a debate about attitudes to old furniture, which tends to be either thrown away or, in the case of "designer" items, treated as icons and hidden away in museums. Dixon wanted to celebrate the fact that Artek's furniture continues to be used in a normal way many years after it was first manufactured.

Cork Furniture

Date **2002**

Designer **Jasper Morrison**

Half of the world's cork is produced in Portugal, where forests of cork oak trees supply the global markets for wine bottle corks, flooring tiles, and other products made from this renewable material. Cork comes from the bark of the trees; it is stripped every nine years without damaging the trees. The trees can live for up to 200 years, and each harvesting produces enough material for 4,000 bottles of wine. Portugal alone produces $1 billion worth of the bottle corks each year.

However, the rise of plastic corks and screw-top wine bottles has sent alarm bells ringing through the Portuguese industry, which employs 16,000 people and ensures that vast areas of countryside are both economically productive and sustainably managed. Cork producers fear the forests will die if demand for the material dries up.

Starting in 2002, industrial designer Jasper Morrison has created a series of furniture pieces made from cork, highlighting the beauty of a material not usually used for this purpose and drawing attention to the plight of the cork industry, although Morrison did not have this objection in mind when he designed the series. His first design was the 2002 Cork table and stool, a matching pair of pill-shaped objects for Dutch brand Moooi. The 2004 Cork Family (shown here) was a series of low tables for Swiss brand Vitra made of turned, agglomerated cork. Agglomerated cork is a material made from chunks of cork offcuts that are glued and pressed together.

In 2007 Morrison created a more adventurous chair from the material. His Cork chair for Vitra is a limited-edition piece made from recycled wine-bottle corks. The used corks are pressed into a solid material that is then shaped by a computer-controlled milling machine to create the distinctive chair. Cork has properties that make it suitable for furniture manufacture, since it is light, tough, and soft to the touch. Over time, unsealed cork develops a beautiful dark patina. As the Cork chair proves, the material can also be recycled.

Treasure Furniture

Date **2007**

Designer **Maarten Baas**

There is often a high degree of waste generated during the manufacture of cheap furniture since, when components are cut from sheets of material such as medium-density fiberboard (MDF) or plywood, the pieces left over are simply thrown away. While some designers have tried to create furniture that minimizes the amount of leftover material (see pages 93 and 100), Dutch designer Maarten Baas has instead designed a range of furniture utilizing only the material rejected from a factory.

Baas collects waste MDF from a local furniture factory that produces only a limited number of items in large volumes, meaning the rejected pieces are always the same size and shape. This allows Baas to produce dining chairs and armchairs as unlimited editions. Each batch of furniture produced by the factory provides Baas with enough raw materials to make fifty-eight dining chairs and twenty-three armchairs. He assembles the odd-shaped pieces into his new designs and then paints them, calling the range Treasure, since he is turning something unwanted into something valuable.

Hey, Chair, Be a Bookshelf!

Date **2007, 2006**

Designer **Maarten Baas**

Furniture that has been thrown away by other people is the raw material for a series of designs by Dutch designer Maarten Baas. Baas, who also designed the Treasure range of chairs made from factory offcuts (see page 87), collects unwanted and often broken objects that could not otherwise be sold from secondhand shops and dumpsters, salvaging not only items of furniture but also things such as skateboards, scooters, musical instruments, and toys.

Baas then builds tall sculptural towers up to 98 inches (2.5 m) high from these ingredients, piling up lamp standards, old chairs, and tables and adding violins or vases to create new functional items from the old. The title of the series, Hey, Chair, Be a Bookshelf!, refers to the way that these assemblies suggest unexpected new uses for his finds: chairs can now be used to store books, violins can be used to hang up coats, and lampshades become umbrella holders. Once he has completed an assembly, Baas strengthens it with polyester and finishes it in colored polyurethane.

Paperskin (Plakbanterie)

Date **2007**

Designer **Johan Bruninx**

Damaged secondhand furniture is given a new lease of life in this project by Dutch designer Johan Bruninx. The cracks, dents, and scratches in the surfaces of the unwanted items are covered up with a new surface made of brown paper adhesive tape, which is skillfully applied in patterns that resemble traditional marquetry.

The project, called Paperskin (*Plakbanterie* in Dutch), was presented by Bruninx in 2007 for his graduation show at Design Academy Eindhoven in the Netherlands. Bruninx presented tables, chairs, cupboards, and chests of drawers as part of the project, which demonstrates how ugly or damaged furniture can be reinvented and renewed by simply applying a new surface material.

Bruninx applies the paper tape as if wrapping a precious gift, forming radial patterns that look like fine marquetry designs created using exotic wood veneers. This trompe l'oeil effect camouflages the cheap workmanship or damaged appearance of the original item, but at minimal cost. An unwanted item becomes something new and valuable-looking, extending its life and delaying the point at which it is disposed.

Twig Furniture

Date **2005**

Designer **Russell Pinch**

The flexible but tough wood of the hazel tree has long been valued in England for the long, straight sticks it produces when the tree is coppiced—regularly cut back to encourage new growth. Coppiced hazel is fast-growing, reaching a height of 20 feet (6 m) in five to seven years, when it can be harvested. The trees can live for around seventy years, and when properly managed, coppiced hazel woodland provides a rich habitat for wildlife, making this a highly sustainable crop. Hazel sticks have traditionally been used for making fences and, when bundled together, for repairing riverbanks and building dams.

British furniture designer Russell Pinch had long wanted to try working with hazel, and following a chance meeting with a man who grew hazel trees for these traditional purposes, he was given permission to cut some sticks from the coppicer's woodland to take back to his studio.

The result was Twig furniture, a handmade series of seats made of dozens of stacked hazel sticks. The sticks are first dried, then joined tightly together with concealed metal pins to form long, square-sectioned blocks containing several hundred sticks of different thicknesses. The whole block is then sawed to length, leaving the ends of the branches cut flush. Pinch produces two versions of the seat in different lengths: a 5-foot (1.5 m) bench and an 18-inch (45 cm) cube.

Paper Mâché Armchair

Date **2007**

Designer **Majid Asif**

Papier-mâché—a French term meaning chewed-up paper—is best known today as a children's craft technique, but before the development of plastics it was widely used for making objects such as dolls, storage boxes, and jars. The technique was widespread in China several hundred years ago, while in Russia from the late eighteenth century onwards, objects made from papier-mâché and then lacquered and finely decorated were in vogue. Papier-mâché canoes were common in the United States in the 1800s.

The technique produces surprisingly strong yet lightweight structures, especially when reinforced with textiles. When made with waste paper and natural water-based glue, papier-mâché is an environmentally friendly material.

Old newspapers are the raw material for the Paper Mâché armchair, designed by British designer Majid Asif while a student at University College for the Creative Arts in southeast England. He first exhibited the chair at the New Designers show in London in June 2007.

Asif got the idea from a newspaper article showing products made from used newsprint. To make the chair, he built up 120 layers of newspaper over an inflatable mold, first soaking the paper in wallpaper paste. Once the outer shell had dried, Asif deflated and removed the mold. Each chair is different due to the irregular way in which the flexible mold behaves, and the newspaper pages used to make the chair, which can be read while sitting in the chair.

Non-Woven Furniture

Date **2007**

Designer **Christian Kocx**

Manufacturing processes often produce offcuts of high-quality materials that go straight to landfill sites or incinerators, resulting in a waste of resources and causing environmental problems. It is often not cost-effective for manufacturers to reclaim these offcuts: it is cheaper to buy new materials in bulk than to recycle small amounts of the same material left over from their own factories. Many designers are now turning their attention to these waste materials, since they can often be acquired cheaply and, having been subjected to various processes before being discarded, they often have unique forms that designers can use to create unusual products.

Dutch designer Christian Kocx collects plastic plugs left over from injection molding machines and uses them to create a range of products called Non-Woven. The bowls, lamps, and chairs are all made of plastic remnants that he heat-fuses together in a steel mold. By taking material that would be discarded and turning it into a new product, Non-Woven adopts the same approach as the Treasure furniture by Maarten Baas (see page 87).

Kocx graduated from Design Academy Eindhoven in 2006 and launched his Non-Woven range in 2007 at the Milan Furniture Fair and Dutch Design Week.

Strata

Date **2007**
Designer **Ryan Frank**

Strata is a range of furniture made of wood products salvaged from unwanted office furniture. Designed by Ryan Frank, a South African designer based in London, the range consists of a chair, a stool, a coffee table, and a dining table, all manufactured by Portuguese furniture brand Imadetrading. The range gets its name from the way Frank builds up the pieces from strips of timber and chipboard taken from old desks, with their visible grain looking like geological strata.

Each piece contains 60 to 70 percent recycled material. The rest is made of birch plywood certified by the Forest Stewardship Council, an international organization that certifies that timber and timber by-products come from sustainably managed woodlands. The plywood is necessary to ensure the structural strength of the furniture. The recycled timber is acquired from Green Works, an environmental charity in the United Kingdom dedicated to reducing the amount of office furniture that ends up in landfill sites. Since 2002, the charity has prevented over 17.5 million cubic feet of redundant office furniture from being dumped, instead refurbishing, recycling, and reselling it.

The Strata range is designed to be as flexible as possible—the chair and stool have integrated storage platforms that can hold items such as books and magazines, while the coffee table can be stacked on top of the stool to save space and provide shelving. The range is a development of an earlier project by Frank. Called Harvey, this was a rocking stool made entirely of waste wood and recycled timber products such as plywood and chipboard. The stool was produced in a limited edition of ten.

Frank's work often relates to the urban environment and tackles issues of decay and degradation. An earlier product called Hackney Shelf features chipboard panels strategically placed around east London, where they attracted the attention of graffiti artists who illicitly decorated them in street art. The panels were then used to create mobile storage units. Another product, Traffic, is a coffee table with a top made from pieces of chipboard that were left lying on the ground where they were driven over by cars and bicycles, developing a grubby patina recording city life.

100 Chairs in 100 Days

Date **2006–2007**

Designer **Martino Gamper**

Part design project and part performance, 100 Chairs in 100 Days is a furniture collection by London-based designer Martino Gamper that was made by reassembling found and unwanted objects into new pieces. As the name of the project suggests, Gamper set himself the challenge of making a chair a day for one hundred days, collecting his raw materials from a variety of sources, including scavenging from dumpsters and dumps and asking his friends to give him their unwanted items of furniture. Returning to his workshop each day, Gamper would take apart his finds—which consisted largely of discarded chairs but also other objects including guitars, baskets, and bicycle seats—and reassemble them into new chairs. The result is a series of one hundred completely different designs, some of which are bizarre hybrids between two different types of chairs and some of which are more akin to abstract sculptures.

The 100 Chairs in 100 Days project was intended as a way of exploring new ways of designing—Gamper was faced with a haphazard kit of parts from which he had to select components, and the making process involved much trial and error. Gamper himself describes the process as "sketching in 3-D" and the speed at which he had to work meant the project was as much an exercise in handcrafting as a kind of production line for nonidentical objects. The resulting chairs, which were sold to a Milanese gallery at the end of the project, are highly evocative, giving strong suggestions of their former lives.

In 2007 Gamper carried out another related project called If Only Gio Knew, which also involved the refashioning of existing furniture. This time, instead of using unwanted objects, Gamper was given original interior sets and furniture from the Hotel Parco dei Principi in Sorrento, Italy, designed by legendary Italian architect Gio Ponti in 1962. In an act of design iconoclasm, Gamper took these icons, cut them up, and refashioned them into new pieces, proving that it is not only junk furniture that can be recycled into new objects.

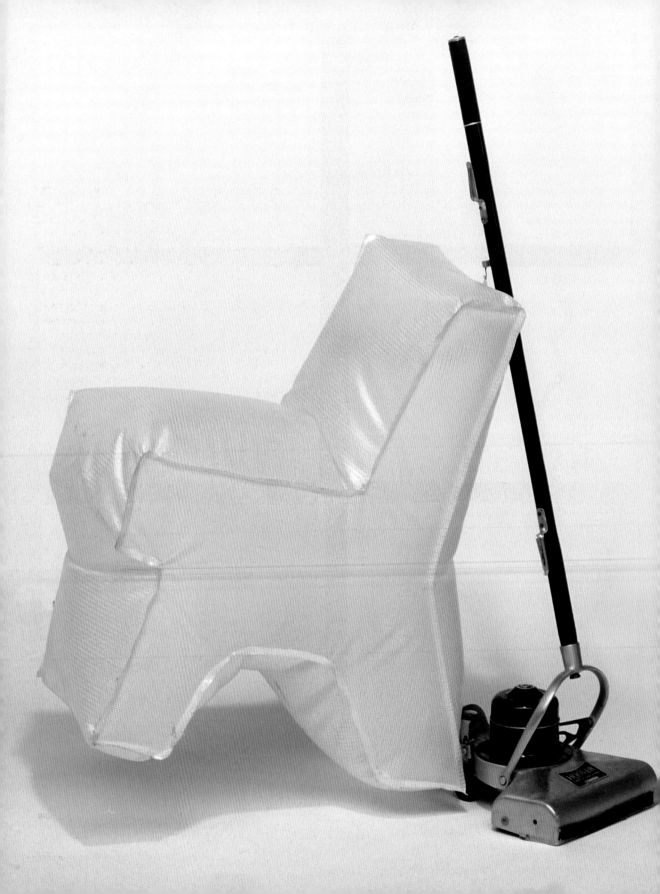

Dust

Date **2004**

Designer **Jurgen Bey**

Dutch designer Jurgen Bey is one of the world's leading conceptual designers, producing objects that are theoretical explorations of contemporary issues as much as proposals for practical objects. His Dust project, which began in 2004, is an ongoing investigation into the possibilities of using materials widely considered to be trash for new purposes. Many other contemporary designers are also working with discarded or worthless objects and turning them into luxurious, handcrafted one-offs—see for example the work of lighting designer Stuart Haygarth (see page 19) or furniture designer Piet Hein Eek (see page 74)—but Bey is unique in proposing furniture created out of household dust, a substance that is as unappealing as it is seemingly impractical.

In a series of exhibitions and installations, Bey has presented prototypes of chairs and other items in the form of vacuum cleaner bags attached to suction devices, so that dust is turned into a comfortable, and cost-free, stuffing material. The project suggested ways in which dust—something that people usually spend a great deal of effort removing from their homes—could serve a useful purpose.

For another project, Bey invited employees of the Forbo linoleum company to bring him the contents of their vacuum cleaner bags. He used this to create a collection of flecked gray patterns that then became designs for a new linoleum range. Bey's thinking in this case was that a floor that was already covered in a dust print would hide additional dirt perfectly and would not need to be cleaned as often.

Dust is typical of Bey's work, which often explores phenomena that nobody else appears to be interested in and that turns accepted notions upside down. In this case, Bey imagines what would happen if dust were to become something that people wanted to keep rather than throw away, and became valuable rather than worthless.

Pano Chair

Date **2008**

Designers **Eva Guillet and Aruna Ratnayake/Studio Lo**

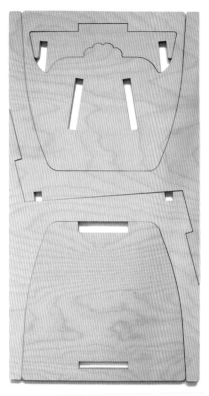

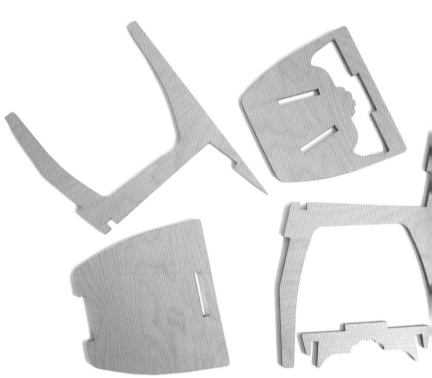

Cut from a single sheet of plywood with virtually no material wasted, the Pano chair by French designer duo Studio Lo—Eva Guillet and Aruna Ratnayake—is an exercise in using resources as efficiently as possible.

The plywood is precision-cut into five interlocking pieces using a water-jet cutter: two identical pieces form each side of the chair, including the legs; another piece forms the seat; a fourth piece makes the back; and a fifth provides structural rigidity beneath the seat. The pieces simply slot together using mortise and tenon joints without the need for glue, screws, or nails, and the only material wasted is where rectangular slots are cut out of the plywood to enable assembly.

Besides minimizing the amount of material thrown away, the Pano chair can be transported cheaply and easily as a flat board and then assembled on arrival.

This desire to use flat sheets of material as efficiently as possible has become a minor trend among contemporary designers. In particular, in 2007, Design Academy Eindhoven graduate Evelien Valk showed an oak secretary made of a plank of oak cut in such a way as to use every part of the timber without waste, while in 2003, British designer Ben Wilson launched a self-assembly chair called Chairfix, made from parts milled from a sheet of MDF that is delivered as a flat board and then put together by the user.

Grownup Furniture

Date **1970s to now**

Designer **Christopher Cattle**

Harnessing nature so that products can be "grown" rather than manufactured has long been a dream of many designers, who foresee the day when the wastefulness of the production process is replaced by the efficiency of growing organisms. In this way, objects could be harvested much like crops. Scientific advances already allow the medical industry to culture or clone materials in laboratories, although research into making products in this way is in its infancy.

The honeycomb vases by Tomáš Gabzdil Libertiny of Studio Libertiny, which are fabricated by bees in a hive (see page 53), give an indication of how this field of research might develop. Dutch designer Joris Laarman, meanwhile, has created a range of designs called Bone furniture in a project that mimics the way bone tissue grows to create chairs and tables that look as if they could have evolved, rather than having been manufactured. However, Laarman's designs are not actually grown but rather are created on a computer and then fabricated in aluminum or resin.

British designer-craftsman Christopher Cattle has been experimenting with a far simpler way of growing furniture since the 1970s. His method involves training three growing tree saplings over a plywood jig and grafting their branches so that they fuse to create a stool that can be harvested after a few years. The stools, which take around five years to reach maturity, are stronger than traditionally joined wooden items and require no glue or fixings, except to join the seat, which is made of turned wood. Since they are grown outdoors, they do not require any additional effort once planted besides occasional checks to ensure they are forming correctly, and they are therefore entirely organic. The grafting techniques used have been practiced by gardeners for centuries.

Each stool has its own character and is peculiar to the location it was grown in, and Cattle claims the lengthy growing process encourages patience—something that is at odds with the instant gratification demanded by contemporary consumer culture—as well as creating a strong affinity between the end user and the object, since the future owner can watch their future product slowly taking shape.

Pallet Furniture

Date **2006**

Designer **Nina Tolstrup**

Pallet furniture is a range consisting of a chair, a lamp, and a stool, made—as the name suggests—from timber salvaged from used pallets. The collection was developed by Nina Tolstrup, a Danish-born designer based in London, for an exhibition exploring issues of sustainability held at the 100% Design trade show in London in 2006. The exhibition, called Ten, invited ten designers to create products using materials found within six miles (10 km) of their studios, and with a budget of just £10 ($19 in 2006). The aim of the show was to encourage both designers and the public to look again at contemporary throwaway culture and instead seek creative ways of making attractive, long-lasting products from humble materials.

Tolstrup's response was to cannibalize timber from the pallets on which goods are stacked in warehouses, allowing them to be moved by forklift trucks. She went a step beyond the exhibition brief by drawing up a set of instructions that allow consumers to build the items themselves; the instructions could be bought from Studiomama—Tolstrup's design studio—for £10.

By encouraging users to make their own furniture from items they find themselves, Tolstrup is following in the footsteps of other designers including Dutch designer Tord Boontje (see pages 14 and 46), whose 1998 Rough and Ready project featured a range of furniture made of everyday items that people could construct themselves. Boontje supplied instructions showing how to make the pieces, thus allowing people to acquire well-made products as cheaply as possible.

Tolstrup's Pallet chair uses the wood of two pallets plus fifty screws, while the Pallet lamp is made out of one pallet, fifteen screws, a bolt, some reused wire, and a light socket. The Pallet stools are made of eighteen end blocks from pallets, which are glued together.

IOU Design for Charity

Date **2008**

Designers **Gabriella Gustafson and Mattias Ståhlbom/TAF Arkitektkontor**

Launched at the Stockholm Furniture Fair in 2008, this range of garden furniture aims to be both environmentally and socially sustainable. The timber range, consisting of chairs, tables, a stool, a bench, and a storage chest, is the first collection by IOU Design for Charity, a new brand based in Sweden. The collection was designed by Swedish architects Gabriella Gustafson and Mattias Ståhlbom of TAF Arkitektkontor, who have attempted to create furniture that will last a lifetime and so never need replacing. Made of Siberian larch, the pieces are naturally resistant to wind and water and do not require surface treatment.

Larch is a material that has long been used in Sweden for humble furniture, but in recent years it has gone out of fashion as more exotic timbers have been marketed to the public. This range is intended to help rehabilitate the extremely durable timber, with the products being sold as sturdy heirlooms that can be passed down from generation to generation rather than as fashion statements, which is how much contemporary furniture is presented. The chair seats and backs and tabletops use planks of varying widths, meaning that as much of the tree as possible is used, reducing waste. IOU is also attempting to ensure that the transportation of raw materials and finished products is as sustainable as possible.

IOU is a charitable foundation and its product development, production, distribution, administration, marketing, and sales departments are set up as educational projects to help marginalized people rejoin society. Business profits are used to help other organizations working to relieve human suffering. In particular, IOU collaborates with the Swedish arm of CRIS (Criminals Return into Society), an organization that helps convicted criminals and drug addicts reintegrate. Through CRIS, these people are given access to IOU's educational and training programs.

Textiles & Materials

The last few years have seen dramatic advances in material and fabric technology, but designers at the greener end of the spectrum appear to be ignoring these in favor of simple, low-tech solutions and rediscoveries of past techniques. Many are making materials themselves, harnessing natural processes, or using recycled substances in what amounts to a return to a craft-based cottage-industry approach to design rather than an industrial approach.

Young Dutch designer Greetje van Tlem, for example, has discovered a way of hand-spinning used newsprint into yarn, from which she makes rugs, curtains, and even clothing. She thus transforms a waste material into a bespoke product that is yet streaked with discernible words and pictures from forgotten newspapers, reminding the viewer of its origins. Catherine Hammerton adopts a similar approach, painstakingly compiling wallpaper designs using found objects such as stamps, bits of lace, and images cut from vintage catalogs, or from the decorative patterns found printed on the inside of old envelopes. Alyce Santoro weaves fabric from unwanted raw materials, in her case taking discarded audiotape to create cloth that can be "played" to reveal the secrets of the original recording in her Sonic Fabric. With his Recycled Icons, Eco-Couture collection, creative director Gary Harvey takes existing clothing and salvaged materials including newspapers and

plastic bottles and recombines them to make statements about the wastefulness of the garment industry.

All these designers share sensibilities with designers from other fields, such as furniture and lighting, who are also turning away from designers' traditional fascination with industrial production and manufactured materials and instead finding delight in transforming everyday raw materials with their own hands. Greetje van Helmond does this too, making exquisite jewelry from nothing more than sugar, which she grows into large crystals in tanks of sugar solution.

Other designers are encouraging nature to do their work for them. Elsbeth Joy Nielsen has found a way to allow silkworms,

usually killed in the traditional silk-making process, to survive by encouraging them to weave small panels of silk before making their cocoons. These delicate panels can be sewn together into scarves and other items while the silkworm pupae are left to metamorphose into moths and continue their life cycle. Jelte van Abbema, by contrast, works with microbes, printing sheets of paper with a substance on which the microbes can feed and multiply. This creates darkened areas, revealing images and words formed by living organisms instead of ink. Both these projects hint at a possible future whereby instead of exploiting the world's natural resources, humans work in harmony with them.

Grão

Date **2007**

Designers **Rita João and Pedro Ferreira/Pedrita**

This project by Portuguese designers Pedrita utilizes surplus tiles from the Portuguese tile industry, taking reclaimed, end-of-line, and discontinued stock and using them to create large murals that can reproduce photographic images.

For the Grão project, Pedrita, which consists of Rita João and Pedro Ferreira, collects used tiles and digitally scans them to record information about their color and tone on a computer. Once they have chosen the image they want their mural to display, they feed it into the computer, which selects the optimum combination of tiles to recreate the image. The tiles are then assembled and fixed in position in the traditional way. Each tile effectively acts in the same way as a single pixel in a digital image, and while the mural is an unreadable jumble of mismatched tiles close up, from further away a clear and faithful image can be seen.

Portugal is home to a large tile-manufacturing industry, and the country has a strong tradition of using tiles to decorate buildings both externally and internally. This project shows how otherwise unwanted tiles can be combined to produce striking collages that can be used architecturally. Grão was first demonstrated in an exhibition at the Portuguese National Tile Museum in Lisbon in the summer of 2007. The tiles, all unwanted designs from the 1960s, 1970s, and 1980s, were all bought from Cortiço & Netos, a large Portuguese architectural ceramics dealer. João and Ferreira systematically documented all the tiles in the company's vast archive, photographing and scanning examples of each design in order to have enough different colored tiles to be able to recreate any image as a mural.

Unsustainable

Date **2007**

Designer **Greetje van Helmond**

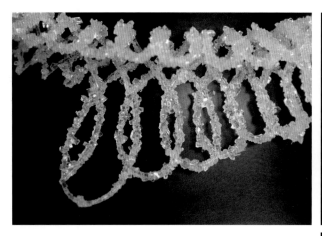

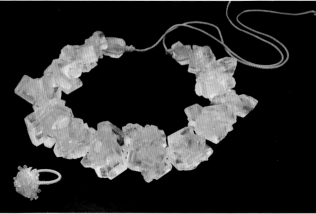

Jewelry is most often made from precious metals and stones, but for this collection, Dutch designer Greetje van Helmond chose to make it from one of the cheapest and most readily available materials she could think of: sugar.

Created for her graduation show at the Royal College of Art in London in 2007, the project is a comment on contemporary consumption patterns, where valuable materials are used to produce objects that are used briefly and then thrown away. Van Helmond has turned this paradigm upside down, creating jewelry—luxury items that are usually cherished for a long time—and making them so fragile that they can only be worn once.

Van Helmond's necklaces and bracelets are created by suspending threads in saturated sugar solution. Sugar crystals form naturally on the threads, increasing in size the longer they are left to grow. It can take several weeks to grow the largest crystals. The photograph on the right shows a necklace growing in a large glass test tube; the pipe and retort stand are just for show and do not play a part in the process.

When removed from the sugar solution, the finished results appear as precious and delicate as the finest handmade jewelry, and indeed the smaller crystals are so fragile that they crumble to the touch, although the larger crystals are more robust. The collection is called Unsustainable, partly because of the short life span of the pieces and partly as a comment on consumer culture. Van Helmond hopes the project will make people think about ways of making precious objects without having to use up nonrenewable natural resources, and will show how the most ordinary natural materials can produce the same effect when used carefully.

Sonic Fabric

Date **2000**
Designer **Alyce Santoro**

Woven from unwanted audiotape, Sonic Fabric is a recycled material that can be "played"; the sounds recorded onto the tape can be heard.

In 2000, Brooklyn, New York–based artist Alyce Santoro began collecting used audiocassettes and experimented with knitting and crocheting the magnetic tape into fabric. She was inspired by childhood memories of being on her father's sailing boat, which had strips of cassette tape tied to it to indicate the direction of the wind. She imagined that the sounds of the tape were being blown through the air, much as Tibetan Buddhists believe that prayers printed on cotton prayer flags are dispersed on the wind.

When Santoro later discovered that the fabric could be played by running a tape head from a cassette recorder over the fabric, she started to produce fabric from tapes she had recorded herself and which contained music that was important to her. In 2004 she custom-made a sonic dress for her friend, percussionist Jon Fishman of the band Phish, who wore and "played" the outfit live on stage in Las Vegas, using specially made gloves with tape heads woven into them.

The project grew, and Santoro first outsourced the weaving to a small family-run mill in Rhode Island and later to a craft cooperative run by Tibetan women refugees in Nepal, as it was Tibetan culture that helped inspire the project. Santoro sends the women audiocassettes, which they then weave into products such as handbags.

In 2006, Sonic Fabric was put into production by giant American textile company Designtex. The commercial fabric features tape mixed with cotton and is still woven at the small Rhode Island mill, although it is now created from large spools of unwanted audiotape that would otherwise go into a landfill. The fabric is apparently durable and comfortable, being breathable and softer than it appears. The Designtex Sonic Fabric was launched at the International Contemporary Furniture Fair in New York City in 2006, where it won best new fabric.

North Tiles

Date **2006**

Designers **Ronan and Erwan Bouroullec**

North Tiles are an innovative, flexible system of fabric-covered foam tiles for interiors that allows internal spaces to be divided without the need for building and demolishing walls. The tiles are also produced according to strict environmental guidelines governing the materials and production methods used. They are designed by French designers Ronan and Erwan Bouroullec for Danish textile manufacturer Kvadrat.

Kvadrat is a company that makes much of its environmental credentials, signing up to the European Union's Flower eco-label (a voluntary scheme that encourages companies to adopt greener practices) and being certified for both ISO-14001 and ISO-9001

environmental management quality standards. It also abides by the Danish Environmental Protection Agency's list of undesirable substances—a register of some two hundred environmentally damaging chemicals and substances—and its transport companies are required to have their own environmental policies in place.

The North Tiles are designed to be self-hanging, fitting together by a system of folding tabs and notches so that they can be suspended from a ceiling or wall. They were originally designed for Kvadrat's Stockholm showroom, to showcase the company's color range. Consisting of two pieces of fabric pressed onto foam blocks,

the tiles can be made in any color and can be configured in an endless variety of ways. Besides allowing the internal configuration of a space to be changed easily without the need for structural work, the tiles have good sound-insulating properties.

In their flexibility, North Tiles are similar to two earlier products by the Bouroullec Brothers: Algue, a system of lightweight plastic branch-like forms that snap together to create internal partitions; and Twig, molded plastic clips that can be assembled to create hanging screens. All three products offer new ways of changing interior spaces quickly and easily with reusable, lightweight components.

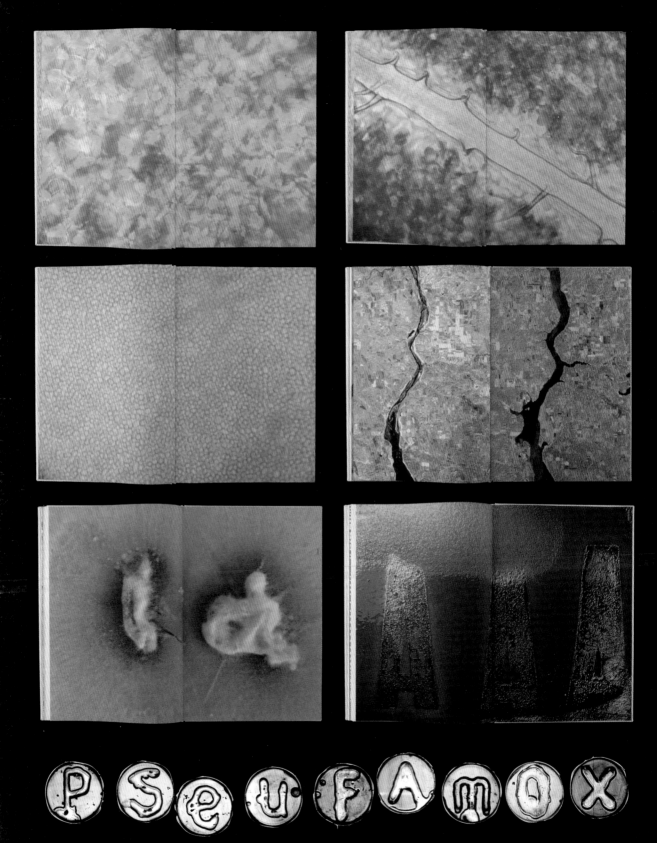

Symbiose

Date **2006**

Designer **Jelte van Abbema**

Scientific advances in fields such as genetic engineering suggest that living organisms will increasingly be manipulated to produce useful raw materials through natural processes. Contemporary designers are beginning to mirror these advances in their own work, exploring how new scientific methods could alter the way objects are created. Dutch designer Jelte van Abbema has explored the possibilities of printing on paper without using chemical-containing inks. He has developed a way of printing with bacteria, breeding them on controlled parts of the paper so that words and images emerge as they multiply.

Van Abbema developed the Symbiose project in 2006 for his graduation show at Design Academy Eindhoven in the Netherlands. He took a course in microbiology at Wageningen University to learn about bacteria and the conditions required to grow them: they prefer a warm, damp environment and are most readily cultivated on agar, a gelatinous substance on which the microbes thrive. Using a harmless,

pigmented microorganism that changed color as it grew, he printed the agar and bacteria onto uncoated paper, using both screen-printing and woodblock printing techniques to ensure the bacteria were confined to the correct areas of the paper.

The paper was then left in a sealed humid environment, and an image gradually emerged as the bacteria multiplied. For his final project, he converted an advertising display box on a bus stop into a giant petri dish to hold a large sheet of bacteria-printed paper. Over the following days, the blank sheet of paper turned into a poster containing a giant letter A in an ever-changing pattern of colors as the bacteria grew, used up all the available food, and then died.

Van Abbema is not suggesting that harmless bacteria could replace ink in the printing industry, but the Symbiose project does hint at the way nature could in future be harnessed to provide environmentally friendly manufacturing methods.

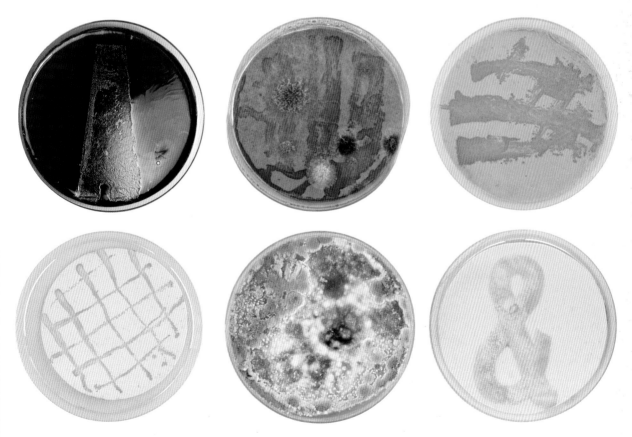

Indruk

Date **2007**
Designer **Greetje van Tiem**

Dutch designer Greetje van Tiem has found a novel way of recycling old newspapers: she spins them into yarn that can be woven into fabric. Van Tiem presented the project as her graduation show at Design Academy Eindhoven in 2007, calling the project Indruk, which means "print."

To make the yarn, van Tiem cuts newspaper into narrow strips and spins it into a thick thread on a traditional spinning wheel. She does not use anything else in the process as the twisting that the paper undergoes gives strength to the yarn, although chemical coatings could be added afterwards to provide fire resistance or color fastness. Each newspaper page can produce 65 feet (20 m) of yarn, and the printed words and images are still visible on the finished thread, serving as a reminder of its origin. Van Tiem has used the yarn to create various textiles, including rugs, curtains, and upholstery. Despite being made purely from old newspapers, the fabric is surprisingly water-resistant and durable.

Van Tiem is one of many young designers experimenting with ways of turning waste materials into beautiful and unexpected new products. Paper and cardboard accounts for roughly 40 percent of household waste, although recycling rates are rising; in Australia, for example, around 75 percent of newsprint is recycled—the highest rate in the world, according the Australian Publishers National Environment Bureau. Some of this paper is chemically de-inked and mixed with virgin wood fibers to make new newsprint, although most is used to make cardboard and pulp-based packaging products such as egg boxes. Newspapers tend to be printed on fairly low-grade paper made of pulp from timber offcuts mixed with between 20 and 40 percent recycled fibers.

Handmade Wall Coverings

Date **2005, 2007**
Designer **Catherine Hammerton**

Young British designer Catherine Hammerton makes luxury handmade wall coverings in limited editions, often using vintage items sourced from antique shops or found objects to add delicate layers of detail to her designs. Her work has much in common with that of other young London-based furniture and lighting designers such as Stuart Haygarth and Committee, who also celebrate the beauty of objects that other people throw away. Hammerton applies similar principles to her two-dimensional work, which includes soft furnishings and fabrics as well as wallpapers.

Hammerton's Collection series of wallpapers (right), launched in 2005, features silk-screened designs finished with vintage fabrics and trims plus elements such as stamps and cutouts from old magazines. Her Victoriana range features hand-printed paper with added hand-stitched birds cut from vintage wallpapers and lace.

The Blossom panel (below), developed in 2007, is a wall hanging made from waxed-paper saucepans, similar to those used in fast-food restaurants but which have been dyed, pierced, and stitched to give them a delicate beauty. Flutter, also from 2007, is a three-dimensional wall covering made from the insides of old envelopes cut to resemble ginkgo leaves and stitched to a wallpaper base so the flaps hang free.

Silk Story

Date **2007**
Designer **Elsbeth Joy Nielsen**

Sericulture, the cultivation of silkworms for the purpose of producing silk, has been practiced for thousands of years and has its origins in China. Yet traditional silk-making involves the killing of the silkworms before they are able to transform into moths. Young Dutch designer Elsbeth Joy Nielsen has developed a prototype for a new, more sustainable method of silk-making that allows the silkworm to complete its life cycle.

Under commercial sericulture, silkworms—which are the larvae of the *Bombyx mori* moth—are fed with mulberry leaves until they are ready to pupate, at which point they spin a protective cocoon of raw silk thread, which is secreted by the salivary gland. Each pupa produces a single thread of up to 984 yards (900 m) in length, and when it is ready to emerge from its cocoon, it secretes an enzyme that dissolves the thread so it can escape. This would render the silk useless for commercial purposes, so before this happens, the cocoon is dropped in boiling water, killing the pupa and making the thread easier to unravel.

Nielsen developed her alternative silk production method while a student at Design Academy Eindhoven in the Netherlands. When the silkworms are ready to begin spinning their cocoons, Nielsen places them onto a cardboard platform with raised edges, which is attached to the top of a stick. The silkworms crawl around the platform looking for a suitable place to make their cocoon, leaving a trail of raw silk as they go. As the caterpillars cross and recross the platform, the silk threads overlap and bond to form a fine mesh.

Once the silk panel is ready, Nielsen removes the caterpillars and allows them to create their cocoons in a suitable place, emerging later as moths to breed and start their life cycle again. The silk panels, meanwhile, are used to make delicate scarves (right) and other products.

Recycled Icons, Eco-Couture

Date **2007**

Designer **Gary Harvey**

During the last century, clothing has gone from being something that was repaired and handed on from person to person to something that is today widely considered disposable. According to the U.S. Environmental Protection Agency's Office of Solid Waste, every American discards more than 68 pounds (31 kg) of clothing and textiles per year, representing 4 percent of all municipal solid waste.

In 2007, as a comment on the waste levels and lack of recycling in the garment industry, London-based designer Gary Harvey presented a collection made entirely of recycled clothes, fabrics, and other materials. Nine outfits were shown at the Estethica exhibition during London Fashion Week, including a wedding dress made of ten salvaged bridal gowns. Each dress makes a distinct point about waste in the industry. Harvey's Baseball Puffball dress (below), made of twenty-six used nylon baseball jackets, is a comment on the way advanced textiles used to make high-performance sportswear have entered mainstream fashion, resulting in nonrecyclable, nonbiodegradable items being discarded at the end of a season. The Black T-Shirt Dress (right) is made of thirty-seven cheap, logo-printed tops—given away by brands to promote their products, and often made in sweatshops by poorly paid workers—cut up and handstitched into a long draped sheaf dress. Denim Dress (far right) is constructed of forty-two pairs of used Levi's 501s, a comment on the way that a garment originally designed as a long-lasting item for workers has become a fashion item that is often discarded in favor of the latest silhouette; while Laundry Bag Dress (below right) comprises twenty-one checked laundry bags made of recycled plastic formed of recycled plastic bottles.

Harvey, a former creative director at Levi Strauss, is now expanding his collection under the brand name Recycled Icons, Eco-Couture.

Products

The environmental conundrum faced by designers is most apparent in the field of product design. Today's global economy relies on ever-increasing demand for products—an inherently unsustainable situation that inevitably means ever-increasing consumption of resources and growing pollution as more and more factories open to meet demand. When working for big companies, product designers are often at best only able to mitigate the situation by reducing the raw materials that go into their products, the amount of power they consume, the packaging they are shipped in, and so on.

Reducing the power consumption of electrical goods has become a goal of many manufacturers recently, as consumers become sensitized to rising electricity prices. Enterprising designers have spotted a niche here, coming up with a host of self-initiated products that monitor the consumption of other goods in the home to make consumers more aware of how their electricity bills accumulate. Wattson, by British designers DIY Kyoto, is one such device, showing on its LED display the accumulated cost of energy consumption in the home.

Big manufacturers have generally been slow to explore ways of greening their products, while many companies stand accused of "green-wash"—trumpeting nonexistent environmental credentials in an attempt to boost their reputations and sales. But as consumer awareness rises, brands are gradually

responding. Sandy Eco by industrial designer ChauhanStudio is a version of an existing domestic telephone designed to be as green as possible, with a shell made of recycled plastic and in recycled packaging.

Manufacturers generally have to produce huge quantities of goods to justify the high costs of setting up production lines, but the rise of rapid prototyping technologies raises the possibility that goods could be created on demand at the location where they are required. Reduced Carbon Footprint Souvenirs is a concept that explores this, suggesting a scenario whereby a traveler could send gifts to friends back home electronically rather than by post.

Despite globalization, a large percentage of the world's population still lacks basic amenities. Many designers feel compelled to address this situation with products designed specifically for the developing world. This chapter includes a range of humanitarian products such as Solar Bottle by Alberto Meda and Francisco Gomez Paz, a bottle that decontaminates water using only the power of the sun.

But the most celebrated product for the developing world is One Laptop Per Child. Designed by Yves Béhar for the half-billion people in the world without electricity, it could revolutionize education in poorer nations and shows that designers potentially have a huge role to play in improving lives.

Rings of Life

Date **2007**
Designer **Jori Spaa**

The jewelry industry involves turning precious metals and stones into objects of desire, with the rarity of the raw materials used being in direct proportion to their cachet and price. This series of sterling silver rings combines contemporary silversmithing with an environmental sensibility, replacing the traditional cut diamond, ruby, or other jewel with something not usually regarded as rare or precious: a seed.

Dutch designer Jori Spaa first showed his Rings of Life (Levinsringen) series at the Design Academy Eindhoven graduation show in 2007. Inspired by the often ingenious ways that plants hold and release their seeds, each of the ten handmade rings features seeds, or a single seed, held in an enclosure with a release mechanism, within a form that relates to a particular species. Rose, for example, features a rosehip held in a spike-shaped container reflecting the thorns that protect roses, while Poppy holds dozens of tiny poppy seeds in a pepper pot–type vessel. Dandelion is in the form of a miniature French horn, through which the user can blow to disperse the parachute-topped seeds. Spaa has also designed Onion, in which the seed is held in thin silver rings that must first be peeled away.

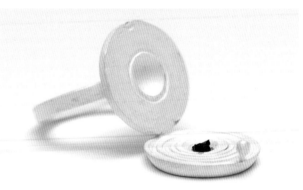

Thus Spaa's rings contain both emotional and environmental messages. The owner (or receiver) of one of his Rings of Life is able to mark a special occasion by releasing the seeds, potentially creating new life in the process—an act that has obvious symbolic connotations. But the rings also refer to contemporary concerns over the loss of plant species, and specifically to ambitious conservation projects that are attempting to collect and preserve for future generations seeds from all the earth's plants. Spaa cites as an inspiration the Spitzbergen Seed Vault in Norway—a giant refrigerated storehouse cut into the side of a mountain on the Norwegian island of Spitzbergen in the Arctic Ocean. With scientists fearing that up to 100,000 plant species are under threat from climate change, overexploitation, habitat loss, and the invasion of alien species, the seed bank, which started receiving seeds in 2007, aims to serve as a "doomsday book" of threatened species.

A similar project in England, the Millennium Seed Bank, aims to preserve seeds from 25 percent of the world's plant species by 2020, in a purpose-built building in West Sussex. Holding the rarest and most potentially useful species, the seeds will be held as in insurance policy against future extinction and will also provide plant material for research.

Sweet Disposable

Date **2003**

Designer **Emiliano Godoy**

Many products are only meant to be used for an extremely short time before being thrown away. Yet unless they are biodegradable or recycled, these disposable items often end up in a landfill: a product that is used for ten minutes can remain intact for hundreds of years.

To counter this growing problem, Mexican designer Emiliano Godoy has investigated the potential of using sugar—a natural material that is harmless and biodegradable—to replace materials such as plastics and ceramics for short-lived products. He has created a range of prototype sugar objects to demonstrate the material's versatility. A table lamp is made of eight identical molded segments; the sugar golf tee can be left on the golf course, where it will harmlessly dissolve; a coat hook demonstrates how sugar can produce durable items. Godoy has also proposed a sugar clay pigeon to replace the traditional ceramic ones, which Godoy claims produce harmful dust when shot.

Sugar is a versatile crop that is farmed for its fibers, for use as animal feed and for fuel (ethanol, a gasoline substitute that is widely used in Brazil, is made of sugarcane), as well as its many uses as a food. Bagasse, the rough fibers left over after processing, is also used as a fuel—especially to provide power for sugar mills—and for making paper and packaging. Every 220 pounds (100 kg) of cane grown yields between 88 and 110 pounds (40–50 kg) of cane juice, which is processed to produce molasses and refined sugars.

Sugar is often cited as a carbon-neutral material, but some estimates suggest that three times more fossil-fuel energy is used to grow, transport, and process the sugar crop than is derived from it.

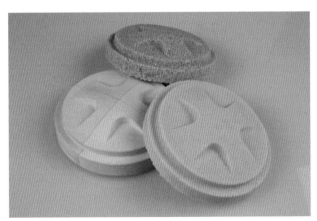

Whole House-Off Switch

Date **2007**

Designer **Jack Godfrey Wood**

Even when not in use, many electrical devices continue to consume power. Standby modes, originally developed to conserve power, have encouraged people to leave devices on rather than switching them off. A survey carried out by Germany's Federal Environmental Agency and the Federal Ministry for the Environment estimated that 11 percent of all domestic energy was consumed by devices in standby mode, accounting for the output of two power stations every year and causing 1.5 percent of the country's greenhouse gas emissions. Another study carried out by the California Energy Commission calculated that 93 percent of the energy used by domestic audio systems was drawn when they were not in use.

Whole House-Off Switch, designed by British designer Jack Godfrey Wood, is a prototype device capable of turning off all nonessential electrical equipment in a home to save electricity. Consisting of a push switch in the form of a graphic representation of a house, the device can be activated on leaving home both for safety reasons—to prevent fire caused, for example, by a heater or iron left on by mistake—and on environmental grounds.

The switch is only a concept at the moment and is not yet being manufactured, but the media attention it has received has helped draw attention to domestic energy waste. However, the debate about electrical goods left on standby mode has two sides, with some arguing that constantly switching devices such as computers and televisions on and off consumes more power and reduces their life span. Others say that if standby modes were removed, consumers would simply leave devices on at full power all the time.

Godfrey Wood has also designed another product designed to raise awareness of energy consumption. Called £used (Fused), this is a system of electrical plugs with screens on the reverse that display the estimated annual cost of running the device they are attached to. The plug displays the projected cost on an E-Ink screen, used because it is easy to read and uses very little power.

Power-Aware Cord

Date **2005**

Designers **Anton Gustafsson and Magnus Gyllenswärd**

Power cords that carry electricity to and from lights and other devices are usually intended to be as invisible as possible, made of black plastic and hidden away. Power-Aware Cord takes the opposite approach. The cord is embedded with electroluminescent wires that glow blue when electricity is passed through them. By glowing with varying intensity, in pulsing or flowing patterns, the light displayed by the cord acts as a visual metaphor for the electricity flowing through the cable, serving as a reminder of the power that is being consumed. Since the electroluminescent filaments glow more strongly when more power is being used, the cord raises awareness of electricity use and encourages the user to moderate their consumption. The cord also acts as an unmissable reminder when a device has been left on accidentally.

The cord was developed by Swedish designers Anton Gustafsson and Magnus Gyllenswärd as part of an energy awareness project called Static! Funded by the Swedish Energy Agency, the project was part of Sweden's Design Year 2005 and saw numerous designers develop products aimed at highlighting energy-use issues. Power-Aware Cord was designed to highlight the fact that since electricity is invisible, consumers rarely think about it and therefore tend to be resistant to the notion of conserving it. Market research carried out with the cord found that people readily associated the blue light with the power that was being consumed, with respondents saying they would find the product useful when educating children about energy saving and when assessing the amount of electricity being consumed by devices operating in standby mode.

Power-Aware Cord is one of the ideas from the Static! project that was taken to prototype stage and into production as a limited-edition product.

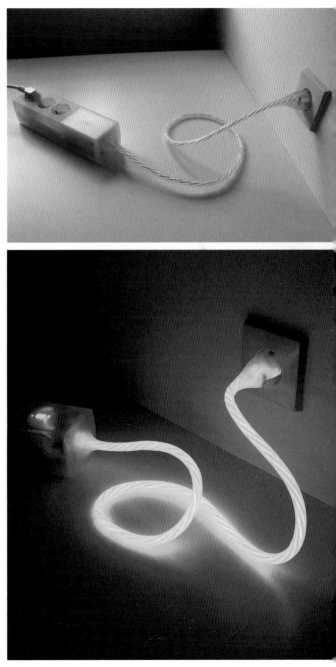

Die Electric Project

Date **2007**

Designer **Scott Amron**

New York City–based Scott Amron describes himself as a "freelance electrical engineer, designer, conceptual artist, and inventor," and this range of prototype products crosses the boundaries of all these disciplines. His Die Electric project is a series of a dozen jokey conceptual designs that are intended to make people think about the amount of electricity they use while proposing alternative uses for electrical fittings in the home.

Each of the products utilizes a standard electrical fitting such as a plug socket, light switch, or bulb holder, but in a way that does not consume electricity. The range takes its name from "dielectric," meaning a material that has negligible electrical conductivity. The simplest, most poetic object in the Die Electric range is a piece of cork with prongs attached that fits into a standard U.S. socket, metaphorically plugging a hole to prevent energy leaking. Likewise,

Amron's GND is a power socket with a green ceramic leaf poking out and blocking the socket, as if the earth itself is pleading against the use of electricity. "Ground pokes through GND," says Amron. "Earth pleads, 'Please don't use this outlet.'"

Candull, meanwhile, is a wax candle with a screw fitting attached to the bottom so that it can be used to replace a lightbulb in a task lamp. As long as the lamp has an articulated head that can be turned upside down, it can be turned into a holder for a less-polluting light source. Other products utilize plug sockets as holders for towels, plants, fire extinguishers, and even toothbrushes, while another item called OFF is a modified light switch with a coat hook in place of the switch. Hanging a coat or other item on the hook pulls the switch to the downward position and turns it off, thereby encouraging people to save electricity.

Biobot

Date **2007**
Designer **Jule Jenckel**

With concern mounting over the future availability and security of fossil-fuel reserves, as well as the environmental issues surrounding the burning of coal, oil, and gas, the search is on for alternative energy sources. This project by German designer Jule Jenckel, created while she was studying at the Royal College of Art in London, explores the potential of microbial fuel cells—sources that harness the power produced when microbes break down food into chemical and electrical energy. Microbial fuel cells, or MFCs, can run on foods such as glucose, acetate, or even wastewater. Scientists have already developed primitive gastrobots: robots that are powered by food. Chew Chew, for example, is a train-like robot developed at the University of South Florida's College of Engineering that moves around on wheels and is powered only by sugar cubes.

As is often the case with scientific developments, MFCs and gastrobots are relatively unknown to the general public, partly because they are difficult to understand and do not look very interesting. With her Biobot project, Jenckel has attempted to take these areas of scientific research, combine them with advances in bioengineering, and give them a physical form that makes it easier to understand how they might be used in the future.

Jenckel's Biobots are bioengineered stomachs that could be grown in laboratories and then used as small portable power sources. Once topped up with sugar, meat, alcohol, or other waste foodstuffs, the Biobots would produce modest amounts of electricity via standard cables and sockets; several Biobots could be linked together when more power was needed. The devices need to be cared for like pets, since they would be living organisms. While being a serious attempt to explore future energy sources, Biobots are also intended to provoke discussion about whether such technologies are acceptable or desirable.

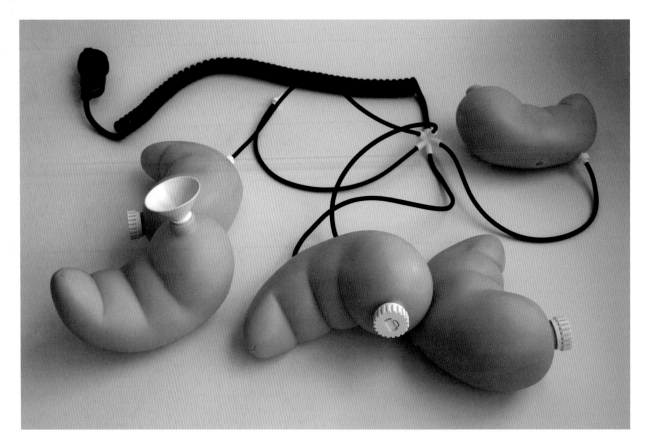

Ventilator

Date **2007**
Designer **Steven Kessels**

Recalling the slow-turning ceiling fans used in the colonial tropics, Steven Kessels's Ventilator is a romantic deconstruction of a product that is usually operated effortlessly with the flick of a switch. The fan runs on human power rather than electricity, but instead of relying on a servant to operate it, the user must spend time and energy turning a hand crank before they can benefit from cooling breezes.

Young Dutch designer Kessels created Ventilator for his 2007 graduation show at Design Academy Eindhoven in the Netherlands. It consists of a ceiling-mounted fan made of timber blades, modeled on airplane propellers. These are turned by a steel driveshaft that runs across the ceiling and down the wall to a series of large gear wheels. A hand crank on one of the wheels lifts a stack of weights towards the ceiling on a rope and pulley; when the crank is released, gravity pulls the weights towards the ground, which drives the wheels in reverse and turns the fan. A few minutes' labor will set the fan turning for an hour or more. Adding more weights to the stack makes the fan turn faster.

Kessels's motivation for the project was a love of old machinery, which was often visible to the user. In contrast, the workings of most products today are hidden within a casing. Kessels believes the workings of cogs and pulleys are beautiful and should be seen. By not requiring electricity or fuel, the fan also makes a comment on our contemporary addiction to power-consuming gadgets.

Bel-Air

Date **2007**
Designer **Mathieu Lehanneur**

Air quality inside homes is often worse than outdoors. Clothing, furniture, electrical goods, and cleaning products all emit pollutants that can be harmful to health; plastics used in furniture manufacture, for example, emit chemicals including benzene, formaldehyde, and trichloroethylene, the last two of which are known carcinogens. Warm temperatures and humidity make emissions worse.

To address this problem, French designer Mathieu Lehanneur teamed up with scientist David Edwards of Harvard University to create an air-filtration system that utilizes the natural purifying effect of plants. The result, called Bel-Air, is a glass and aluminum container that acts as a miniature greenhouse for plants known for their ability to remove contaminants from the atmosphere. A fan draws air into the container and is then filtered by the plant's leaves and roots before being ejected. The humid bath in which the plant sits acts as a third filter. Unlike other air-purifying systems, there is no filter to change and dispose of since the chemicals are absorbed and neutralized by the plants themselves.

The design is based on research carried out by NASA in the 1980s, following concerns about the health of astronauts confined in orbital stations for lengthy periods of time where they were exposed to toxins off-gassed by the fabric of the space station. NASA identified several plant species that were particularly effective at removing toxins from the air, including gerbera, philodendron (a member of the arum family), spathiphyllum (peace lily), pathos (a type of ivy), and chlorophytum (a genus that includes the spider plant).

Bel-Air was created for an exhibition at Le Laboratoire cultural space in Paris in 2007, and it is scheduled for production in 2009.

Post A Phone

Date **2007**

Designer **Paul Priestman/Priestman Goode**

Post A Phone takes a familiar item—a landline telephone—and reengineers it to be as small and as green as possible without sacrificing its functionality. Invented by British industrial designer Paul Priestman of Priestman Goode, the prototype product's casing is made of recyclable cardboard or plastic and, at less than a quarter inch (4mm) thick, it is small and thin enough to fit inside a standard 8.5 x 5.5-inch (A5) envelope.

Besides the savings in transportation costs and packaging (the phone comes inside a thin cardboard folder which also contains instructions) that such a small and lightweight object entails, the designer claims the phone has social benefits: because it can be mailed through a mailbox, the recipient does not have to wait at home for a delivery or visit the local sorting office to collect it.

The phone is designed to serve as a backup unit in case the user's main phone breaks down. The designers feel that despite the rise in mobile phones and data communications, there is a whole generation of people who are more comfortable with landline voice calls. Since even the most basic telephone these days tends to be a sophisticated and complex electronic device, the risk of them malfunctioning and leaving the user stranded is relatively high.

Post A Phone is designed to be as simple as possible to use, having just basic call and receive functions and a clearly marked keypad with nothing but numbers and essential functions. Users can add graphic stickers to keys that can be used to store important numbers, such as family members or the doctor. It simply plugs into a standard phone line and can be used immediately. While the product is something of a novelty and partly intended to be used for marketing purposes, Post A Phone nevertheless highlights the way that modern phones, like many other consumer electronic goods, have become unnecessarily complex yet are often viewed as nothing more than fashion accessories to be thrown away and replaced.

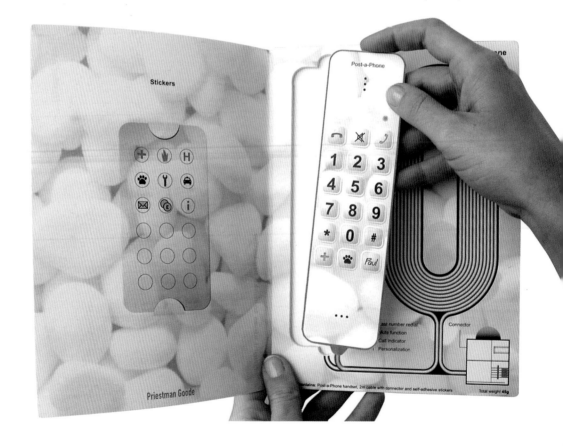

E-Wash

Date **2007**
Designer **Levente Szabó**

Laundry detergents have come a long way since the 1960s, when American manufacturers vied to produce the longest-lasting suds. The chemicals that produced the suds soon made their way into watercourses, leaving rivers, lakes, and even the foot of Niagara Falls choked with detergent foam. Yet contemporary laundry detergents still contain harmful chemicals and pollutants, most notably phosphate, which can cause algal blooms in rivers and lakes. These remove oxygen from the water, killing fish and aquatic plants.

An entirely natural cleaning agent, soap nuts are the small round fruit of a tree that grows in many parts of the world and which have long been used in countries such as India and Nepal for their cleaning properties. They are already being sold in the West for use in conventional washing machines: a porous bag containing a few of the nuts is placed in the drum of the machine instead of detergent. But E-Wash, designed by Hungarian student Levente Szabó, is a washing machine designed specifically for the nuts, and it features a container that ensures the nuts are added to the wash at the right time.

Szabó claims that 2.2 pounds (1 kg) of soap nuts would last the average person a year, reducing the amount of transportation required as well as reducing the need for conventional detergents. E-Wash is also much smaller and thinner than traditional machines but is able to take a similar load, making it more appropriate for smaller homes. Szabó designed E-Wash while a student at Moholy-Nagy University of Art and Design in Hungary, and won first prize in the Electrolux Design Lab 2007—an annual design prize for environmentally friendly products.

Eco Pro Torch

Date **2007**

Designers **John and Tony Davies/Trevor Baylis**

British inventor Trevor Baylis is a pioneer of green industrial design. In 1997 his Freeplay clockwork-powered radio went into production, becoming arguably the first global icon of sustainable design. Powered by turning a hand crank that wound a clockwork mechanism, the original radio ran for up to an hour after just twenty seconds of winding and became a hit not just in the developing world, for which it was designed, but in the developed world as well, where it became a common sight in garden sheds and garages. Baylis originally developed the radio to give people in communities without electricity access to information that would educate them about the AIDS virus, which was beginning to spread rapidly throughout Africa in the 1990s. The radio's social sustainability credentials were enhanced when Baylis set up a factory in Cape Town, South Africa, employing disabled workers to assemble the product.

Baylis's company, Trevor Baylis Brands, now manufactures a growing range of wind-up gadgets, including radios, bike lights, phone chargers, and a media player. The Eco Pro Torch was designed by inventors John and Tony Davies, who brought their idea to Baylis.

The flashlight, which doubles as a mobile phone recharger, is based on technology similar to that in Baylis's other products, although in this case the hand crank mounted on the flashlight powers three rechargeable nickel-metal hydride (NiMH) batteries. These batteries, which come in standard AA and AAA sizes, are more environmentally friendly than lightweight nickel-cadmium (NiCd) batteries, which contain poisonous cadmium. The nickel from NiMH batteries can safely be recovered and recycled at the end of the batteries' life. The batteries are charged by winding a foldaway hand crank mounted on the device: sixty seconds of winding will power the torch for around twenty minutes, or provide about two minutes' talk time on a mobile phone. The product has zero primary emissions, meaning it emits nothing during use by the consumer.

Reduced Carbon Footprint Souvenirs

Date **2007**

Designer **Héctor Serrano**

Transportation accounts for around one-third of the world's greenhouse gas emissions. This conceptual project by Spanish designer Héctor Serrano investigates ways of reducing the need to ship goods from place to place, proposing instead to send digital descriptions of objects via email to three-dimensional printers, which materialize the object at the destination.

Serrano has chosen tourist souvenirs for this hypothetical project, creating a range of ten stereotypical figurines depicting famous sights around the world. Instead of posting gifts to their friends or carrying them home, tourists would select souvenirs and specify messages to be engraved on their bases. A computer-aided design (CAD) file would then be sent via the Internet to a device capable of turning the data into a real object, such as a stereolithography machine. Stereolithography is a form of rapid manufacturing, or "3-D printing," a technology that converts a digital file into a solid object made of plastic or metal. This relatively recent technology allows extremely

complicated objects to be fabricated and is widely used to make prototype components for the car and medical industries. Objects are made in a single stage, meaning the process is theoretically more energy- and time-efficient than traditional production lines, which involve complex assemblies of many different parts.

As 3-D printing technology develops, the prices of the machines is falling to the extent that experts foresee a time when domestic 3-D printers will be as common as inkjet printers. Indeed, 3-D printers work in much the same way as inkjets, building up microscopic layers of material in three dimensions rather than just two.

Serrano developed the project for an exhibition called Ten Again, held at the 100% Design trade show in London in September 2007. The exhibition asked ten designers to each create ten different products exploring sustainability issues. Other projects commissioned for the Ten Again exhibition include Gitta Gschwendtner's Flame lamps (see page 20) and Nina Tolstrup's Pallet furniture (see page 103).

Wattson

Date **2006**
Designer **DIY Kyoto**

Designed to help householders reduce their energy consumption, Wattson is a small portable gadget that monitors the amount of electricity used in a home and displays the accumulated cost of the power via an LED display. The device can show energy consumption in dollars, pounds sterling, or euros, or in watts. The product is designed by U.K. company DIY Kyoto, which consists of three graduates from the industrial design and interactive design courses at the Royal College of Art in London. Wattson was first shown at the Designersblock show in London in 2006 and has since gone into production.

Wattson consists of three parts. A sensor is attached to one of the cables that runs between the electricity meter and the fuse box, measuring the power passing through the wires. The sensor is attached to a battery-powered transmitter, which is hidden out of sight. The transmitter relays information wirelessly to the Wattson

display unit, which can be located up to 328 feet (100 m) away (or 98 feet [30 m] if there are walls in the way). This portable unit is designed so it can be placed in view in any part of the house, providing a constant reminder of how much the homeowner is paying for their electricity. The idea is that this encourages consumers to turn off unused devices and make more efficient use of electrical goods.

Besides displaying electricity-use data, the display unit also features an array of LED lights that change color as power consumption rises and falls. The unit can display up to one month's data, which can be downloaded to a computer and analyzed by Holmes, an accompanying software package that can produce graphs showing daily, weekly, monthly, or annual consumption patterns. Wattson can also be used to measure the power coming from microgenerating devices such as photovoltaic panels or wind turbines.

Local River

Date **2008**

Designers **Mathieu Lehanneur and Anthony van den Bossche**

The environmental damage caused by industrial farming and fishing methods, and the pollution resulting from transporting foods over long distances, is causing many people to investigate ways of sourcing food grown closer to home. This, coupled with concerns over the freshness and purity of foodstuffs, has led to movements such as farmers' markets, where growers from the surrounding countryside set up stalls in urban areas, and groups such as the "locavores"—a San Francisco movement of people who only eat food produced within 100 miles (160 km) of where they live.

Local River, by French designer Mathieu Lehanneur (see also Bel-Air, pages 132–33) in collaboration with Anthony van den Bossche of Duende Studio, is a response to these concerns. His conceptual product is a combined domestic aquarium and fish farm that also grows vegetables; fish and greens cohabit for a short time in the unit before being eaten by their keepers. The product is based on principles of "aquaponics"—the symbiotic cultivation of fish and plants, with plants used to absorb nutrients from fish waste that would otherwise build up in the water and make it toxic to the fish. The result is less pollution and environmental degradation. Aquaponic methods have long been used by farmers in the Far East, where fish waste is used to fertilize fields and fish are sometimes bred in flooded rice fields. The principles have recently been investigated and taken up more widely, particularly by small-scale growers.

First exhibited in New York City in 2008, Local River is conceived for the domestic market, with small tanks used to breed freshwater fish such as tilapia or perch. Edible plants such as lettuce would be grown in pots that sit on top of the tank. To make his design appear more visually pleasing than your average fish cultivation tank, Lehanneur proposes making the product from blown and thermoformed glass.

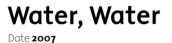

Water, Water

Date **2007**
Designer **Ines Sanchez Calatrava**

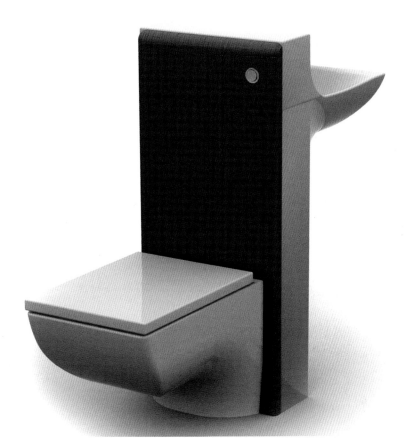

Every person in the Western world consumes an average of 42 gallons (160 l) of water per day. Approximately 13 gallons (50 l) of this total is used to flush the toilet. Spanish designer Ines Sanchez Calatrava has responded to this statistic with a proposal for a combined washbasin and toilet, which uses "gray" water from the basin to fill the toilet tank. Sanchez Calatrava calculates this would save up to 3 gallons (12 l) per person per day, representing a saving of up to 1,320 gallons (5,000 l) per year.

Her concept, which was developed while she was a student at Ravensbourne College of Design and Communication in the U.K., aims to create a symbiotic relationship between two domestic items that have hitherto been considered separate. This approach could be extended to other household appliances, Sanchez Calatrava believes; for example linking the shower with the washing machine or dishwasher. Sanchez Calatrava's inspiration comes from observing

that it is easier to waste water than to conserve it. When a tap is on, water is automatically wasted. Saving the water by inserting a plug into the waste pipe requires an action, but allowing running water to pour directly into the drain does not. Water, Water is partly intended to challenge this attitude, although Sanchez Calatrava hopes to put the design into production. She proposes a modular design so that elements can be changed to vary the style of the unit, and points out that adoption of her design would simplify the plumbing in domestic bathrooms, since only one set of pipes would be required.

Many believe that access to fresh water will be one of the key challenges in the future, in the Western world as well as the developing world. Only 3 percent of all water on Earth is freshwater, of which two-thirds is frozen as ice in glaciers and the polar ice caps. Just 0.3 percent of water is surface-lying freshwater, of which seven-eighths is found in freshwater lakes such as the Great Lakes in North America.

LifeStraw

Date **2005**

Designer **Mikkel Vestergaard Frandsen**

Like Solar Bottle (see page 153) and Aquaduct (see page 159), LifeStraw is another product designed to render polluted water safe to drink. This product, however, is designed for use where there are no reliable water sources such as wells or standpipes—a reality for many of the estimated 1.1 billion people around the world who do not have access to safe water. Some six thousand people die every day as a result of diseases carried by water, most of them children.

Designed by Mikkel Vestergaard Frandsen, who heads Danish emergency response and disease control company Vestergaard Frandsen, LifeStraw is a lightweight tubular device that allows surface water found in puddles and pools to be safely drunk. No training, electrical or mechanical power, maintenance, or spare parts are required, and there is no waiting involved: the user simply submerges one end of the device in water and drinks from the other, drawing water through the product's filtration system by sucking.

LifeStraw, which costs around US $3 per unit to produce, measures just 10 x 1 inches (25.4 x 2.5 cm), and is small and light enough to be worn around the neck. The straw's outer shell is made of high-impact polystyrene. The filtration system uses a specially developed halogenated resin to kill bacteria and viruses on contact, while an activated carbon filter removes iodine and improves the taste of the water. The makers claim the device removes 99.99 percent of parasites and bacteria and 98.7 percent of waterborne viruses. Each LifeStraw can purify around 185 gallons (700 l) of water—enough to last one person around a year—before it must be replaced.

Since being launched in 2005 the product has won multiple awards, including *Time* magazine's Best Invention of 2005; *Esquire* magazine's Innovation of the Year prize, 2005; and the Saatchi & Saatchi Award for World Changing Ideas in 2008.

Q-Drum

Date **1994**

Designers **PJ and JPS Hendrikse**

Many of the humanitarian products in this book have been created by First World designers for the developing world, but the Q-Drum is a device developed in Africa for Africans.

According to the World Health Organization, just 47 percent of rural Africans have access to clean piped water and only 43 percent have sanitation, leaving them vulnerable to waterborne diseases such as cholera and dysentery. Many villagers have to walk miles to reliable water sources, and Q-Drum, a cylindrical water container with a hollow center that can be rolled along the ground like a tire is designed to make collecting water quicker and easier. By passing a rope through the void, the container can be dragged along, making it far easier to transport water than other containers that have to be carried.

The product was designed in 1993 by South African architect Hans Hendrikse and his civil-engineer brother Piet, and the first version, which could hold 13 gallons (50 l), was launched in 1994. Since then a larger version has been introduced that can hold 20 gallons (75 l). The drum, which measures 14 x 19.5 inches (35.5 x 49.5 cm), is made from quarter-inch-thick (4 mm) rotation-molded Linear Low Density Polyethylene (LLDPE) and is built to be virtually indestructible. It can survive a 10-foot (3 m) drop when filled with water and will withstand compression of up to 4 tons (3.7 tonnes)—equivalent to being at the bottom of an 82-foot (25 m) stack of filled containers. During extensive field-testing, a prototype Q-Drum travelled 17,456 miles (2,000 km), making seven million revolutions and providing water for a family of thirteen. During the twenty-month test, the drum only experienced 0.02 inches (0.5 mm) of wear, meaning the product should withstand ten years of hard use. The drum has no moving parts apart from the plastic screw-on cap. The product is designed to be stacked up to forty units high. The Q-Drum is in daily use in about a dozen African countries.

XO Computer

Date **2006**

Designer **Yves Béhar**

Most of the two billion children in the developing world receive inadequate education, according to the One Laptop Per Child project, with just one in three reaching the equivalent of fifth grade. Half a billion have no access to electricity.

One Laptop Per Child (OLPC) was established in 2005 by computer scientist Nicholas Negroponte to develop a sophisticated yet simple-to-use and affordable computer that would transform the learning opportunities of children in developing nations. The result, which went into production in 2007, is the XO, better known as the $100 Laptop, as that is the intended goal price. Negroponte, founder and former head of the pioneering Media Lab at the Massachusetts Institute of Technology, unveiled the first laptop prototype in November 2005; it featured a distinctive yellow crank handle that allowed it to be powered by hand. The final design, created by Yves Béhar of San Francisco–based design company Fuseproject, was launched the following year, with the iconic hand crank replaced by two "rabbit-ear" antennas. When flipped up, these instantly connect the laptop to the Internet and to all other laptops within range via a mesh network.

The computer has many other innovations, all developed to make the product easier and cheaper to use. Its central processing unit is designed to automatically go to sleep between operations, helping the computer to consume just 2 watts—a tenth of a conventional laptop. The dual-mode screen can switch between a standard color LCD screen and a black-and-white "e-book" screen that can be read by students learning in bright sunlight. The computer can still be charged via a crank, now integrated into the external transformer; via a pedal; pull-cord; solar panel; or even a car battery.

Perhaps the XOs most innovative feature is that all its software is open-source, meaning users do not have to buy expensive licensed software. The laptop was launched to great critical acclaim, winning many design awards in its first year. A second-generation computer, a notebook with two touch screens replacing a keyboard and traditional screen, called the XOXO, was launched in 2008.

Sandy Eco

Date **2008**

Designer **Tej Chauhan/ChauhanStudio**

Sandy, an affordable cordless telephone aimed at the domestic market, was launched in 2005 by Hong Kong communications company Suncorp. The phone featured a large handset with a reduced keypad that sat in a block-like base station.

Three years later, the brand launched Sandy Eco, an updated version that looks almost identical to its predecessor but which is designed to be as environmentally friendly as possible. Designed, like the first Sandy, by London-based designer Tej Chauhan, Sandy Eco's handset is made of 100 percent recycled ABS plastic. The phone features software called ECO mode, which the manufacturer claims reduces electromagnetic emissions transmitted between the handset and the base station. The power required to transmit signals between the handset and the base station has been reduced by 50 percent, and Suncorp promises to reduce the base station's power requirements to almost zero in future.

The phone also attempts to reduce the amount of paper and card used in packaging and in the literature that comes with the product. The gift box it is shipped in is made of recycled cardboard while the Quick Start Guide that comes with the phone is printed on recycled paper. There is no user manual in the box; instead, full instructions are available on the Internet.

Printable Offerings

Date **2008**

Designers **Nicolas Cheng and Michael Leung/Studio Leung**

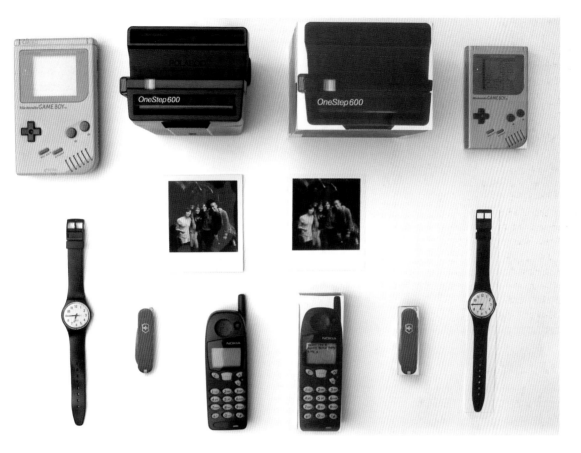

In China it is traditional to burn replicas of everyday items such as televisions and computers as offerings for the dead. The items, which can be bought in specialist shops and supermarkets across China, are burnt at festivals such as Qingming and the Hungry Ghost festival as gifts to deceased relatives. Traditionally these offerings were made of paper, but more recently metallic paper or plastic has been used, potentially creating noxious fumes when they are burned. Printable Offerings, by London designers Nicolas Cheng and Michael Leung of Studio Leung, provides a nontoxic alternative while taking advantage of the potential of the Internet to remove the need to manufacture, transport, and store products.

The designers have created a range of full-size models of popular items that can be downloaded from the Internet and printed on standard paper. The user then cuts out the objects and assembles them into 3-D replicas by folding and gluing the tabs. Printable

Offerings comes with instructions to "print on recycled paper, assemble with solvent-free glue, and burn responsibly."

The first Printable Offerings collection was designed for the Qingming Festival in April 2008—a time when people enjoy the spring and visit the graves of departed ones. The objects include iPhones, notebooks, pens, passports, and wallets, as well as humble items such as packets of tissues and cigarettes. Printable Offerings hints at the future potential of the Internet to replace the traditional mass-manufacturing cycle with products that are made locally on demand. The rise of three-dimensional printing techniques such as stereolithography and other processes known as rapid prototyping (see page 137) potentially allows people to download digital files and then print solid objects at home or at a local 3-D printing facility. In this way, technology allows the manufacturing process to be tailored to individual requirements, thereby reducing waste.

The Beacon

Date **2005**

Designer **Marks Barfield Architects**

Wind power is one of the oldest forms of power generation, having been used for centuries to turn windmills and drive sailing ships across the seas. Today, many designers are exploring ways of maximizing the potential of this abundant source of free power. Most proposals involve clusters of lofty turbines on wind farms in rural areas, or small individual turbines attached to buildings in urban areas. However, the former tend to be controversial, as some people feel they ruin unspoiled countryside and harm wildlife, while the latter do not always perform particularly well due to lower wind speeds and turbulence caused by buildings at low levels in urban areas.

London architects Marks Barfield, best known for the London Eye observation wheel designed for the Millennium celebrations, has proposed a speculative design that is halfway between the two. The Beacon is a 131-foot-high (40 m) Y-shaped structure that supports five vertical "triple-helix" wind turbines, provided by a London-based company called Quiet Revolution. Vertical turbines are quieter than windmill-type turbines and vibrate less. They also do not need to point into the direction of the wind, making them more efficient in turbulent wind. Each turbine on The Beacon is 16 feet (40 m) high and 10 feet (3 m) in diameter.

The Beacon is designed to be located in urban areas where it could be placed along roads, in public spaces, or on rotaries. The height means the turbines are positioned clear of low-level turbulence that adversely affects power generation, and the designers calculate that each structure could generate 50,000 kilowatt hours per year. In addition, they claim that placing the turbines in the areas where power is most needed leads to even greater efficiencies, since between 30 and 50 percent of electricity generated at rural wind farms can be lost because it is transmitted to distant cities.

Public Space Shading Canopy

Date **2006**

Designers **Omid Kamvari, Asif Khan, and Pavlos Sideris**

This product began life in 2006, when a group of students from the Architectural Association School of Architecture in London were invited to take part in a workshop in Recife, Brazil, that discussed ways of creating public spaces such as squares, boulevards, and parks that were appropriate to the tropical city. The students, Omid Kamvari, Asif Khan, and Pavlos Sideris, quickly realized that European notions of public space were not appropriate to the locality, partly because open spaces with stone or concrete paving were too exposed to the fierce sun during the day and were therefore unused. They also noticed that the *favelas*—the slums and shantytowns that are a feature of every Brazilian city—contained no spaces where people could congregate and socialize.

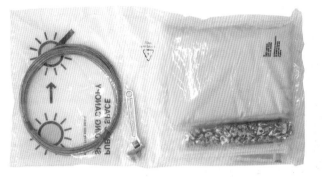

As a result, they devised a product that could quickly and cheaply transform any section of street into a pleasant shaded space. Using only off-the-shelf components and tools—Lycra, brass eyelets, steel cable, cable ties and grips, and a wrench—they developed a simple canopy that could be slung across a street using existing structures such as building façades, water tanks, and utility poles as supports. The total cost of the components was less than $100.

The students then worked with residents of the Favela Do Pilar, a shantytown located between Recife's historic port and the industrial districts, to install the canopy over a busy narrow thoroughfare that served as one of the entrances to the slum. Working without plans or a survey, the team began installing the canopy, negotiating the right to attach the cables with building owners and quickly attracting the help of local people, who brought ladders, tools, and even a music system to help the work along. In the four hours it took to install the canopy, the number of people using the street increased, with schoolchildren stopping to chat with their friends and workers eating their lunch. Local people continued to care for the canopy after the students had left, repairing and adapting it. The bright yellow fabric was visible beyond the *favela*, acting as a beacon and a source of pride.

The team later developed the canopy as a product that could be bought and adapted for use anywhere in the world.

4:Secs Condoms

Date **2007**

Designer **Roelf Mulder/…XYZ Design**

Condoms can play an important role in reducing the infection rate of HIV/AIDS and other sexually transmitted diseases, yet people are often reluctant to use them for a variety of social and cultural reasons. In addition, the misapplication or use of damaged condoms can allow the transmission of disease, yet another reason to defer use.

The 4:Secs condom has been developed to overcome the stigma and embarrassment of applying a condom manually, in the hope that this will lead to greater condom usage and thus help reduce the spread of HIV/AIDS. Designed by Roelf Mulder of the Cape Town industrial design studio …XYZ Design, each condom comes with an integrated applicator that dramatically speeds up the time it takes to put on, and reduces the chances of breakage or damage caused by fingernails during application. The applicator is a two-piece plastic ring that contains the rolled condom. To apply the condom, the user grips the lugs on either side of the applicator between the thumb and

forefinger of each hand and draws the condom over the erect penis with a single movement. Once the condom is fully unrolled, the two parts of the applicator come away and can be discarded.

Mulder has been refining the design for several years, developing the first-generation design in 2001 and later marketing it under the Pronto brand name; the first-generation applicator is part of the permanent collection at the Museum of Modern Art (MoMA) in New York City. The condoms were rereleased in 2007 under the brand name 4:Secs—a double entendre referring to the purpose and speed of the design—complete with racier packaging.

South Africa has the worst rates of HIV/AIDS infection in the world, with UNAIDS, the Joint United Nations Programme on HIV/AIDS, estimating that around 5.5 million people were living with the virus and 320,000 died AIDS-related deaths in 2005. Almost 20 percent of people aged 15 to 49 are infected with HIV/AIDS.

Creative Review Green Issue

Date **2007**

Designer **Peter Grundy/Creative Review**

In April 2007, *Creative Review*—a monthly U.K.-based magazine that covers visual design and advertising—put out a special edition that analyzed its own environmental impact. Called the "It's About Time We Did Something About Sustainability and the Environment" issue, it came without a cover—saving 8,700 sheets of cover-stock paper in total. The first page combined the contents with a large graphic image of a foot by information designer Peter Grundy, representing the magazine's monthly carbon footprint, calculated to be 1.3 tons (1.17 tonnes) per edition.

The eighty-four-page issue contained a feature auditing the resources that go into a typical edition of the magazine, starting with the question: "It's all very well doing an issue about sustainability, but isn't publishing a magazine one of the most environmentally unfriendly things that you can do?" The audit found that each print run of around nine thousand copies consumed almost 239,000 square yards (200,000 sq m) of paper, 53 gallons (200 l) of ink, 1.5 gallons (5.8 l) of chemicals, 49 pounds (22 kg) of glue and—to make the plates

from which the magazine is printed—242 pounds (110 kg) of aluminum. The plates are melted down and recycled after each issue, saving enough electricity to power an average household for 131 days.

The feature also pointed out that of the 820,120 tons (744,000 tonnes) of magazines produced in the U.K. in 2006, more than half—57 percent—went to landfill. Twenty percent were archived, and 23 percent—including the 45 percent of all magazines printed that are never sold—were recycled. According to the magazine, the U.K. paper industry has the best recycling record of any industry sector, with 68 percent of its raw materials coming from waste paper each year. However, a study quoted found that the U.K. was the fifth largest per-head consumer of paper and cardboard in the world, with the average person consuming 458 pounds (208 kg) per year. The United States topped the table, with 688 pounds (312 kg) per person.

In an attempt to learn from its audit and reduce waste, *Creative Review*'s green issue came in a biodegradable polywrap, and some of its pages were printed on 100 percent recycled stock.

Shell Burial Urn

Date **2008**
Designer **LOTS Design**

Shell, by Swedish industrial design group LOTS Design, is one of several recent designs that reexamine the way that people are buried or cremated. Burial is perhaps the ultimate form of recycling, as it is the point when a human body is returned to the soil after a lifetime on earth. There is no reason, designers are saying, why this process should not be subjected to the same industrial design analysis as other human activities.

Shell is a container made of pressed paper that is designed to hold cremated ashes. After the funeral ceremony, the ashes are placed in the container along with messages or personal objects, which can be placed in a pocket built into the top of the object. Friends and family can also write messages to the deceased on the surface of the shell, which has been designed to be dropped into the sea where the paper will gradually dissolve until there is nothing left.

Shell is similar in concept to Bird Feeder, a product designed in 2006 by British designer Nadine Jarvis. Made of human ashes mixed with bird food and beeswax, the objects are designed to be hung from trees, where birds would gradually consume both the food and the remains until all that is left is a wooden perch inscribed with details of the deceased. Jarvis has also designed a set of pencils with leads made from the carbon contained in cremated human remains. The average body produces enough ash to make 240 pencils—a lifetime's supply of pencils for those left behind. The pencil sets are called Carbon Copies.

Another industrial design company exploring ways of making funerals more sustainable is EcoCoffins, a British company that designs and makes coffins from 90 percent recycled paper and card. The biodegradable coffins can be decorated by friends and relatives of the deceased before being buried.

Solar Bottle

Date **2007**

Designers **Alberto Meda and Francisco Gomez Paz**

An estimated one-sixth of the world's population do not have access to safe drinking water, making them vulnerable to waterborne diseases including cholera, typhoid fever, hepatitis A, and dysentery. Diarrhea alone kills an estimated 2.5 million people every year.

Solar Bottle, by Italian designer Alberto Meda and Argentinian Francisco Gomez Paz, is a container that uses the power of the sun to disinfect contaminated water and render it safe to drink. The product employs a system called SODIS, or Solar Disinfection System, which uses the heat and radiation in solar energy to destroy the pathogenic microorganisms in water that cause disease. Solar Bottle is designed to maximize the effect of the SODIS system, which does not require chemicals or special equipment but instead relies solely on the disinfectant qualities found in sunlight.

The transparent 1-gallon (4 l) bottles are made of PET (polyethylene terephthalate), the same type of plastic used to make bottles for branded drinking water. Flattened to maximize the amount of sunlight that can fall on it, the bottle has a transparent side that is oriented towards the sun. The other side is backed with reflective aluminum, which helps increase water temperature inside the bottle. The carry handle folds back to act as a stand, which helps orient the bottle correctly. To be effective, the bottle should be placed in direct sunlight for six hours, or two days if the sky is cloudy. This should be enough time for the UVA radiation in sunlight, combined with a rise in the water's temperature that increases the disinfectant qualities of the radiation, to make the water safe. If the water reaches a temperature of 122 degrees Fahrenheit (50 degrees Celsius), the process can take just one hour.

Solar Bottle won first prize in the Home category of the 2007 Danish Index Awards—a biennial awards program that rewards designs that substantially improve important aspects of human life.

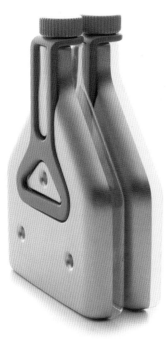 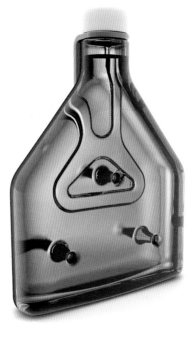 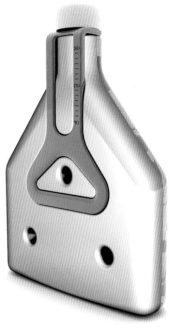

Transportation

Since mechanized transport replaced horse-drawn vehicles early in the last century, humans have overwhelmingly relied on fossil fuels to propel them around the world with increasing ease and speed. Yet with sharply fluctuating oil prices, concerns over future fossil-fuel supplies, and mounting opposition to the environmental impact of carbon-spewing cars, airplanes and seagoing vessels, the transportation industry recognizes that dramatic changes may be required in the next few years.

The automobile sector in particular is on the verge of dramatic changes. Large manufacturers, aware that the gasoline era cannot last forever, have been investigating alternatives such as hydrogen, biofuels, and electric vehicles for years. Hybrid cars, which employ both an internal combustion engine and an electric motor to improve fuel efficiency and reduce emissions, are already a reality. The Toyota Prius, introduced in 1997, was the first commercially available hybrid. The success of the Prius has led other brands to push forward with their own plans. Honda recently became the first major manufacturer to introduce a commercial hydrogen-powered car, the FCX Clarity, which runs on hydrogen fuel-cell technology and produces no harmful emissions.

BMW already runs a demonstration fleet of cars powered by internal-combustion engines adapted to run on liquid hydrogen. Other manufacturers are experimenting with electric cars. Seymourpowell's design for the ENV motorcycle, meanwhile, brings fuel-cell technology to the realm of two-wheelers.

Many designers dream of harnessing the power of the sun to propel vehicles—Ross Lovegrove has proposed a solar-powered bubble car called Car on a Stick and a Swarovski Crystal Aerospace concept car that runs off solar panels, while teams entering the Panasonic World Solar Challenge in Australia have already proven that vehicle-mounted photovoltaics can propel specially designed cars over vast distances. Commercial solar-powered cars are still a long way off, but waterborne vehicles such as the Serpentine Solar Shuttle in London show that solar power can be viable even in places without a sunny climate.

In air travel, there are as yet no realistic green alternatives to jet engines, so manufacturers are instead trying to make their passenger planes as light and efficient as possible, as in the case of the Boeing Dreamliner, and there is a surge in interest in airship technology, which promises ecofriendly travel over long distances, such as Jean-Marie Massard's Manned Cloud.

Another emissions-free mode of transport that is enjoying a renaissance is the bicycle, particularly thanks to bike-sharing schemes like the Vélib' and Bicing projects, and commuter-friendly folding bikes such as the Strida. The runaway success of these projects suggests that persuading people to leave their cars at home and walk or cycle may be the best way for cities to improve the health of their citizens.

Vélib'and Bicing

Date **2007**

Cities **Paris and Barcelona**

The idea of providing free shared bicycles in urban areas has been around since the 1960s, when schemes such as the White Bicycle program in Amsterdam embodied the communal idealism of the age. At its height, hundreds of white-painted bicycles were freely available in the city, with citizens using the bikes for journeys and then leaving them at their destination for the next user. However, many such schemes fell victim to crime and vandalism, and they were abandoned. But as cities struggle to contain vehicle congestion, such ideas are once again becoming popular.

Two of the most high-profile and successful schemes, Vélib' and Bicing, were launched in 2007 in Paris and Barcelona respectively. Vélib' is a contraction of *vélo libre*—free bicycle—while Bicing is on based on a mix of the word *bicicleta*, the Spanish word for bicycle, and BCN, the popular abbreviation of Barcelona.

Although quite separate, the two schemes have much in common. To deter theft, users must first register online and prepay for bicycle rental using a credit card. They can then go to one of the many automatic rental stations dotted around the cities where, upon swiping a prepaid RFID (radio-frequency identification) card, they can unlock a bicycle and ride away. The stations feature rows of bicycles secured to metal rails, with the locking mechanisms integrated into the bicycles. The bike has to be returned to any of the other stations in the city within a set period of time, otherwise a fine is incurred.

Launched in July 2007, Vélib' is owned by the Parisian city authorities and financed by outdoor advertising company JCDecaux in return for a share of the revenue generated by advertisements on the bike stations. Eventually, the scheme will provide twenty thousand bicycles at 1,450 stations. Bicing was launched a few months earlier, in May 2007. Subsidized by car drivers who buy parking tickets in the city center, the project was projected to provide three thousand bikes by 2008, with four hundred stations covering 70 percent of the city.

Strida 3

Date **2006**

Designer **Mark Sanders/MAS Design**

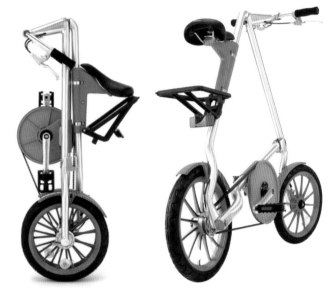

British designer Mark Sanders was inspired by the Maclaren baby buggy when he designed the Strida bicycle, a product that radically reinvents the urban folding bike. As cities seek to reduce congestion by discouraging car use, the folding bicycle is a potentially useful niche product that would allow people to gain the health benefits of cycling, while also being able to hop on and off public transport for longer journeys or to escape bad weather. Folding bicycles can also be brought indoors rather than being locked up on the street, reducing the risk of theft.

Frustrated by the complexity of existing folding bikes and their unwieldiness when folded, Sanders started from scratch, concentrating on designing the simplest folding mechanism possible and ensuring his product could easily be carried onto buses and trains. To achieve this, Sanders reduced the familiar bicycle form to a triangle made of three aluminum tubes that, when folded, create a wheeled

stick that is easy to carry around. The manufacturer claims the bike can be folded in just six seconds. The original Strida design has been improved and updated several times, with the Strida 5 being the latest incarnation of the design.

Strida only has one gear; power is transferred from the pedals to the rear wheel via a greaseless Kevlar belt drive that does not require oil and lasts up to fifty thousand miles (8,500 km). The 16-inch (40-cm) wheels are made of injection-molded plastic and are therefore rustproof, while tires can be changed without removing the wheels.

Sanders has also designed an even more radical and lightweight folding machine called the X-Bike, with a frame consisting of just two carbon fiber tubes hinged like a pair of scissors. Developed for Sinclair Research, X-Bike features a drive belt contained within the frame, a steering system based on pulleys and cables, and extremely small wheels. At the time of writing, X-Bike has yet to go into production.

Aquaduct

Date **2008**

Designer **IDEO**

Part mode of transportation and part water-purification device, Aquaduct is a concept product that was developed for Innovate or Die, a design competition for pedal-powered machines organized by American bicycle brand Specialized and Google.

Since many people in the developing world have to travel a long way to fetch water, and as that water is often unsafe to drink, industrial design studio IDEO came up with the idea of putting a mechanically driven water-purification system onto a bicycle, so that dirty water could be rendered safe as it was being carried back to the rider's village.

Based on the chassis of a tricycle, the three-wheeler features a large water tank over the rear axle into which water is poured.

The tank, the filtration system, and the tricycle's mechanism are all protected by a fiberglass shell. There is a pump attached to the pedal crank that takes in water from the tank as the rider pedals, drawing it through a carbon filter to a second, smaller tank mounted in front of the handlebars. This tank is transparent so the rider can see how much purified water has been collected, and is detachable, meaning it can be carried into the home. The vehicle has a clutch so that more water can be filtered while it is stationary.

The prototype Aquaduct bike was designed and built over a three-week period in late 2007 and was awarded first prize in the contest.

ENV Motorcycle

Date **2005**

Designer **Seymourpowell**

Powered by a nonpolluting fuel cell, the ENV motorcycle is a major step towards tackling transportation's contribution to climate change. The ENV (emissions neutral vehicle), which was launched as a prototype in March 2005, is the first commercially viable two-wheeler to be powered by fuel cells.

Fuel cells convert hydrogen into electricity without creating pollution and have long been regarded as one of the most promising ways of delivering clean energy. The device is virtually silent, and the only by-product of the chemical process that converts hydrogen and oxygen into electrical power is water vapor. Refining the hydrogen in the first place is less environmentally friendly, but taking into account the refining process, fuel cells are estimated to generate just half the pollution of gasoline engines.

Designed by London-based industrial design firm Seymourpowell for British fuel cell manufacturer Intelligent Energy, the ENV has a top speed of 50 mph (80 kph) and a range of 99 miles (160 km). The 6-kilowatt electric engine is powered by a removable fuel cell pod mounted between the handlebars and saddle, which can be demounted and used to power other devices. The manufacturers claim each fuel cell, called a Core, is capable of powering a motorboat or a small home. The bike was designed to show that fuel-cell technology has now improved enough for them to power vehicles. It takes five minutes to refill the 1-kilowatt fuel cell with hydrogen, giving four hours of engine use. A battery pack stores power while the bike is idling or coasting, boosting power when required for acceleration or high speeds.

Fuel cells are not new: they were invented in the nineteenth century by Welsh lawyer Sir William Grove, and NASA developed them further in the 1950s and 1960s. However, recent concerns over climate change, as well as fears about the dependability of global gas and oil supplies, have led to a surge of interest in the technology.

Serpentine Solar Shuttle

Date **2007**

Designer **Christoph Behling/SolarLab**

Designed to ferry passengers across a lake in Hyde Park, London, the Serpentine Solar Shuttle is the latest solar-powered vessel designed by Christoph Behling of SolarLab Research and Design—a studio that is pioneering the use of photovoltaics to power vehicles.

The boat has a curved roof clad with twenty-seven photovoltaic modules that produce 2 kilowatts of electricity to charge batteries, which in turn power two electric motors. This is enough power to propel the 47.5-foot (14.5 m) boat and a maximum load of forty passengers at five miles per hour (8 km/h). The vessel operates in silence, produces no emissions, and can function on cloudy days, while the batteries can store enough power to travel twenty miles (32 km) in darkness should the boat need to operate at night. When not in use, the vessel can act as an energy supplier to the national grid. The designers estimate the vessel will save around 2,900 pounds (1,315 kg) of carbon dioxide emissions per year, compared to a diesel-powered boat of a similar size. It costs around 15 percent more than a conventional boat to build, but fuel savings mean these additional costs should be recouped within three years.

The Serpentine boat is the third solar-powered vessel designed by SolarLab, with similar vehicles already operating in Hamburg, Germany, and on Lake Constance, where it ferries passengers between Germany, Switzerland, and Austria, which all border the lake. A fourth boat will launch on the River Thames in London in time for the Olympic Games in 2012. This will be the biggest solar vessel ever built, capable of carrying 255 passengers.

SolarLab is also developing other vehicle types, including a solar-powered rickshaw. A canopy covered in photovoltaics will provide 80 percent of the vehicle's power requirements, with pedal power providing the rest. The 11.5-foot-long (3.5 m) vehicle will have a top speed of twenty miles per hour (32 km/h) and will save an estimated 2.2 tons (2 tonnes) of carbon dioxide emissions compared with a traditional diesel-powered taxi. A hybrid solar- and hydrogen-powered land train is also being developed for a London park.

Manned Cloud

Date **2005**

Designers **Jean-Marie Massaud and ONERA**

Airships were a popular form of mass transport up until the 1940s, when their speed and capacity became surpassed by airplanes. The 1937 *Hindenburg* disaster accelerated the demise of the airship: thirty-six people died as the hydrogen-filled Zeppelin—the largest aircraft ever built—caught fire when attempting to land in New Jersey.

The return of the airship has been regularly predicted since then, and in the last few years there have been several proposals for the rehabilitation of this majestic means of transport. The use of noncombustible helium instead of volatile hydrogen has removed the risk of another *Hindenburg*-style fire, while designs for luxury vessels akin to flying hotels have kindled hopes of a return to a more elegant and leisurely style of travel. Also, airships—or dirigibles—also require far less energy per passenger than aircraft, which have to burn fossil fuels to keep the heavier-than-air vessels airborne. As public concerns about air travel's contribution to greenhouse gases rise, the airship seems set for a revival.

First mooted in 2005, the whale-shaped Manned Cloud was developed by French industrial designer Jean-Marie Massaud in conjunction with ONERA, the French national aerospace research office. Manned Cloud, which for now remains a concept, has a capacity of forty passengers and fifteen crew. Measuring 689 feet (210 m) long and with a total volume of 18.4 million cubic feet (520,000 m3), the vessel derives its lift from two helium-filled buoyancy tanks while a two-deck cabin suspended beneath them contains cabins and facilities including a restaurant, library, fitness suite, and spa. There is also a sun terrace set above the helium tanks. The vessel has a range of 3,100 miles (5,000 km) and can fly nonstop for seventy-two hours, cruising at eighty miles per hour (130 km/h). Driven by propellers, its top speed is 105 miles per hour (170 km/h).

Helium is commercially extracted from natural gas, which contains around 7 percent helium. The gas is produced naturally as uranium and other radioactive materials decay.

Car on a Stick

Date **2008**

Designer **Ross Lovegrove**

Welsh industrial designer Ross Lovegrove is fascinated with solar power and has developed many speculative projects that harness the power of the sun. Car on a Stick is one of the most fanciful, but also one of the most ambitious, trying to solve many of the problems faced in urban areas simultaneously.

The project proposes a new type of compact urban vehicle that is less threatening and polluting than modern cars. Lovegrove has designed a new urban vehicle that resembles a bubble, with an all-around glass screen and four passenger seats arranged around a central column inside the vehicle. Used for shopping and family outings, the vehicle has no trunk—users instead store their shopping and goods in recesses on the floor.

On the bottom are four small multidirectional wheels that allow the car to move in any direction, while the top of the vehicle features a canopy of photovoltaic panels that drive the vehicle. The friendly, transparent form of the vehicle is designed to bring the occupants

into visual contact with their surroundings, making them part of the street scene and reducing the antagonism that often exists between car occupants and pedestrians; the cars would be lit internally at night for the same reason. The vehicle has no controls, navigating by satellite and voice control.

When not in use, the car is maneuvered onto discs located on the ground. These discs then raise it into the air on hydraulically powered telescopic poles, clearing space at street level for pedestrians while

allowing the car's photovoltaic panels to continue charging. At night, lights on the underside come on, acting as street lighting.

Car on a Stick resembles an earlier project by Lovegrove called Solar Seed. First proposed in 2004, this was a speculative design for a nomadic home, shaped rather like a lightbulb and powered by a solar canopy on the dome-like roof. Solar Seed homes were intended to be placed in the landscape for short-term habitation and could be moved around easily.

Tesla Roadster

Date **2007**

Designers **IDEO and Tesla Motors**

Electric cars are not a new concept, and many vehicles already exist that derive their power from onboard batteries that are charged while stationary. However, these tend to be utilitarian vehicles such as electric milk trucks and golf carts rather than high-performance cars.

The Tesla Roadster, launched in 2007 and styled by design studio IDEO, is the first serious attempt to mass-produce an electric sports car. It is aimed at green-minded drivers who do not want to sacrifice performance. Manufacturers Tesla Motors of California claim the car provides an exhilarating driving experience while producing one-tenth of the pollution of a gasoline-fueled vehicle, and one-third of the carbon dioxide emissions of a hybrid vehicle.

The two-seater, open-top roadster is powered by a lithium ion battery pack that takes around 3.5 hours to charge fully, giving the vehicle a range of about 220 miles (355 km) on a full charge. Since it does not need the fuel, water, and oil lines, combustion chambers, timing belt, clutch, exhaust system, and other elements essential to a gasoline engine, the electric engine is tiny compared with those in normal cars and weighs about the same as a watermelon. However, it can accelerate the vehicle from 0 to 60 miles per hour (0 to 97 km/h) in under four seconds and produces a top speed of 125 mph (200 km/h).

As it is charged from the electric grid, the car is not entirely emissions free, but the makers claim it achieves the equivalent of 125 mpg (53 km/l) of fossil fuel. Efficiency is achieved by reducing the weight of the vehicle to a minimum and by making the motor as efficient as possible, so that power is used to drive the vehicle rather than to generate heat—which is what happens with much of the output of a gasoline engine. A sophisticated computer constantly monitors and adjusts the engine to ensure maximum efficiency, and the vehicle also features a regenerative braking system, which converts energy used to slow down the car back into electricity.

Toyota Prius

Date **2001**
Designer **Toyota**

First introduced in Japan in 1997 and introduced worldwide in 2001, the Toyota Prius has become the best-known and best-selling hybrid car in the world, garnering huge amounts of media attention and helping to make fuel-efficient cars fashionable and desirable. Hybrids are cars that run on both gasoline and electricity, constantly switching between the two power sources to ensure maximum efficiency. On average, hybrids use around 20 percent less fuel than gasoline-only vehicles. They are considered by many to be an interim technology that sits partway between the gas-guzzlers of the past and the low-emission, low energy–consuming electric or hydrogen-powered cars of the future.

Hybrids use a gasoline-fueled internal combustion engine at higher speeds, while electric motors, powered by onboard batteries, take over at low speeds, when the car is reversing or standing still, or to start the vehicle. Sophisticated computers constantly monitor vehicle systems and driving conditions, automatically switching between gasoline and electric power. Hybrids like the Prius also make use of regenerative braking systems, which capture the energy used when braking the car in batteries to provide additional electric power.

The Prius, which is available as a four-door sedan or a five-door hatchback, is among the most fuel-efficient production cars on the road today. An assessment carried out by the U. S. Environmental Protection Agency gave the 2008 model Prius a fuel consumption of forty-six miles per gallon (19.5 km/l), making it the most fuel-efficient car on sale in the United States.

After its introduction in Japan—where sales had been modest—the Prius went on sale in Europe and the U.S., where its adoption by environmentally aware celebrities such as Brad Pitt, Cameron Diaz, and Leonardo DiCaprio helped the vehicle achieve cult status and ensured a long waiting list for the vehicles. The success of the Prius has encouraged other carmakers to introduce hybrids, with Honda introducing hybrid versions of its Civic range in 2005 and Lexus—a luxury brand owned by Toyota—introducing hybrid sedans and a hybrid sports utility vehicle (SUV) in 2006. Many more manufacturers have since announced plans for their own hybrid vehicles.

Honda FCX Clarity

Date **2007**

Designer **Honda**

Honda's FCX Clarity, unveiled at the Los Angeles Motor Show in November 2007, is a family sedan powered by a fuel cell—a device that converts hydrogen into electricity via a chemical reaction instead of combustion, with water being the only by-product. Electricity is stored in batteries and fed into the vehicle's electric motor, which is topped up via a regenerative braking system that harnesses energy used to slow the car. The car's range is 270 miles (435 km), its top speed is 100 mph (160 km/h), and its fuel efficiency is equivalent to 68 mpg (29 km/l).

Other manufacturers are also testing hydrogen-powered cars, including BMW, whose Hydrogen 7 vehicle is powered by an engine that burns hydrogen. However, this vehicle is based on an existing production model, the BMW 7 Series. The FCX Clarity, however, was designed from scratch, meaning it became the first dedicated-production fuel-cell car available to the public in 2008, when a fleet of the vehicles was leased in southern California, a state with strict environmental laws.

The main problem with hydrogen-powered cars is the present lack of refueling points. The vehicles need to be topped up regularly with hydrogen, which needs to be stored under carefully controlled conditions, but by autumn 2008 there were just seventy operational hydrogen fueling stations in the U.S. and Canada, with another forty-one planned. Also, since it takes electricity to produce the hydrogen in the first place, fuel-cell cars cannot really claim to be emissions free unless this electricity is generated from renewable sources. Honda has recently invested in a new factory in Kumamoto Prefecture, Japan, which produces thin-film photovoltaics—a new generation of solar panels that can be manufactured using half the energy of traditional crystal silicon solar cells. The carmaker believes these cells could eventually power domestic hydrogen stations that would extract hydrogen from water and provide motorists with their own supply of fuel for their fuel-cell cars.

Nuna4

Date **2007**

Designer **Nuon Solar Team, Delft University of Technology**

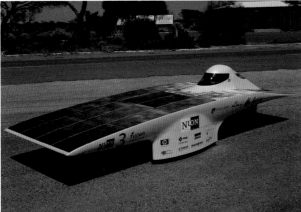

An event held every two years in Australia, the Panasonic World Solar Challenge has become a key event in the development of solar-powered vehicles. Competitors race 1,870 miles (3,010 km) along the Stuart Highway from Darwin to Adelaide in specially built cars powered only by the sun.

The race has led to the evolution of a distinctive type of vehicle that borrows equally from the aerospace and Formula 1 industries: the highly aerodynamic race cars feature large, flat upper surfaces covered in photovoltaic cells that drive efficient electric motors while drivers are enclosed in tiny cockpits that bulge above the fuselage to give a view of the road ahead. Teams have developed sophisticated techniques to maximize power, including making use of the road's camber by driving on the left side of the road in the mornings when the sun is in the east and on the right in the afternoon.

The Nuon Solar Team from Delft University of Technology in the Netherlands has dominated the race in recent years, winning all four races they have entered for since 2001. Nuna3, their entry in 2005, broke the world record for a solar car, averaging sixty-four miles per hour (103 km/h). New rules were introduced for the eleventh race in 2007 because organizers felt the contest's original goal of promoting the development of high-performance solar vehicles capable of traveling long distances at speed had been achieved. Designers were forced to make changes that would make their machines more similar to ordinary cars, including upright driving positions, roll bars, and a maximum 64 square feet (6 sq m) of photovoltaic panels.

Yet Delft won once again, with their Nuna4 design, which averaged fifty-six miles per hour (90 km/h) over the five-day race. The three-wheeled Nuna4 weighs just 441 pounds (200 kg) and consumes as much power as a vacuum cleaner. Its upper surface is covered with 2,318 photovoltaic cells that charge a lithium-polymer battery pack. This in turn drives the rear wheel via a 7.5 horsepower (5.6 kilowatt) direct-drive electric motor.

Loremo

Date **2007**
Designer **Loremo AG**

The heavier a vehicle, the more energy it requires to move, and the less fuel efficient it is. Also, heavy vehicles potentially cause more damage if they crash, meaning extra safety features need to be incorporated, adding further to the weight. This concept car challenges this paradox. The Loremo is intended to be as lightweight as possible to increase fuel efficiency to the maximum while not compromising on safety.

Loremo, which stands for Low Resistance Mobile, has been developed by German company Loremo AG, which plans to put the car into production in 2009. The vehicle weighs just 1,322 pounds (600 kg), less than half the weight of a standard vehicle and about the same as a Formula 1 car. The Loremo does 157 mpg (67 km/l) and in a typical year, driving an average 12,427 miles (20,000 km), it would consume around 105 gallons (400 l) of fuel—a quarter of the amount used by a conventional vehicle. Yet it has a top speed of 160 mph (257 km/h).

The Loremo achieves these efficiencies by paring the car down to a minimum of parts and by rethinking many of the accepted tenets of car design. Instead of side doors, which must be solidly built to absorb impacts and which weaken the rigidity of the vehicle, the Loremo is accessed through a "gate" that swings up at the front. Occupants step over the vehicle's sills to gain access. This device allows the vehicle to be built around a "linear cell structure": a grid of three longitudinal steel struts joined by one cross-strut. Weighing 209 pounds (95 kg), this structure is made of folded sheet steel, making it cheap to produce while ensuring the safety of occupants. Aerodynamics are important to the vehicle's efficiency. The Loremo offers a surface area of just 2.4 square feet (0.22 sq m) to the wind and has an aerodynamic coefficient of 0.20—extremely low for a passenger vehicle.

Boeing 787 Dreamliner

Date **2007**

Designer **Boeing**

Many people would argue that there is nothing green about jet airplanes, and as such air travel has become one of the main targets for environmentalists. According to the Carbon Trust, short-haul flights release around ten ounces (290 g) of carbon dioxide into the atmosphere per passenger per mile—double that of bus travel and three times higher than travel by train.

Long-haul flights are less polluting per mile, generating 6.25 ounces (180 g) of carbon dioxide—a figure that is lower than that of a gasoline car, which emits 10.5 ounces (300 g) of carbon per mile. However, a single 9,000-mile (14,485 km) flight from London to New York produces more than half a ton of carbon dioxide—a similar amount to what the driver of a small car would produce in a year. Air travel currently accounts for around 3.5 percent of global emissions but this figure is set to grow as this method of travel becomes more popular and affordable. In response to passenger demand—and to

airlines' concerns over rising fuel prices—airline manufacturers are now developing more fuel-efficient passenger jets.

Unveiled in 2007, the Boeing 787 Dreamliner is a midsize, wide-body passenger jet that, according to its manufacturers, will use 20 percent less fuel per passenger than similar-sized jets, while also being quieter when taking off and landing. Much of the fuel savings are down to the airliner's lightweight body. The Dreamliner is the first large commercial jet made substantially of composite materials, with 50 percent of the plane—including the wings and fuselage—made of carbon fiber–reinforced plastic. The use of more efficient jet engines contributes the rest of the fuel savings. Other initiatives include the ecoJet concept launched by low-cost airline easyJet in 2007. By using rear-mounted "open-rotor" engines and lightweight materials, the airline claims the jet would be 25 percent quieter and emit 50 percent less carbon dioxide than comparable aircraft.

Interiors

Unlike industrial designers and architects, the interior design profession has until now been on the periphery of the sustainable design movement. Yet interior designers may soon find themselves at the center of the green design debate, since their ability to change the way a space works and feels without the need for demolition and rebuilding means they can significantly extend the useful life of buildings. Since buildings require huge resources to construct in the first place, finding new uses once they are no longer fit for their original purpose has obvious environmental, as well as financial, benefits.

There are plenty of recent examples of how intelligent interior design can bring disused spaces back to life using relatively few new resources. The Hotel Ballymun project in Ireland, for example, established a temporary hotel and arts space in a condemned public-housing block, with the project aiming to draw attention to the wastefulness of erecting then demolishing badly designed housing developments.

In the rip-down-and-rebuild culture of Japan, Sayama Flats by Schemata Architecture Office is highly unusual: the architects have refurbished a run-down apartment complex using as few new materials as possible, leaving in place still-functioning

elements such as kitchens and bathrooms but removing almost everything else.

The Boekhandel Selexyz Dominicanen bookshop by Merkx + Girod lies at the opposite end of the spectrum—a giant permanent steel structure has been built inside an 800-year-old church. Yet the store, which is the latest incarnation of a building that has also served as a market, a beer hall, and a bicycle park, proves that this beautiful structure can be endlessly adapted. Stitch Room by Ronan and Erwan Bouroullec is another example of this approach, allowing people to configure large interior spaces quickly and easily with a kit of reusable fabric components.

The domestic room that looks most set for a green makeover is the kitchen. Appliances such as refrigerators, freezers, and ovens are among the most power-consuming devices in the home; dishwashers and washing machines use large quantities of water. Several young designers, including Alexandra Sten Jørgensen, are beginning to suggest ways of creating kitchens that encourage more sparing use of resources as well as ecofriendly practices such as composting of food waste.

In a sign that this way of thinking might prove commercially viable, appliance giant Whirlpool has developed a "green kitchen" that recycles gray water and promises to halve energy use.

Konstam Restaurant

Date **2006**

Place **London**

Designer **Thomas Heatherwick**

This restaurant, in a converted pub near King's Cross station in London, has been included for its menu rather than its interior design. Opened in 2006 by chef Oliver Rowe, Konstam aims to source all its ingredients from within the Greater London area. By doing this, Rowe wanted to prove it was possible to serve exciting, delicious food without having to fly in ingredients from around the world—a practice that is proving increasingly controversial as supermarkets stock their shelves with fresh produce air-freighted from distant countries.

Rowe's experiment aims to reduce the "food miles" of his dishes to a minimum, since 85 percent of the produce used in Konstam's kitchen is grown and processed within the M25 ring expressway that defines the outer limits of London. The wheat for the bread, for example, is grown in Barnet and Dartford and milled in Ponders End; the bread itself is baked in Wandsworth. Canola oil grown in Epping and pressed in Suffolk is used instead of olive oil, which would have to be imported. Goat's cheese from Chesham and pork from Amersham are also on the menu. Other ingredients, such as wild garlic, nettles for soups, and hawthorn leaves for salads, are foraged in the countryside around London. Rowe admits that he cannot find everything locally, and imported items are clearly marked on the menu, notably wines, which are sourced from France and other countries, although there are several English wines available as well.

The interior was designed by multidisciplinary designer Thomas Heatherwick, using a palette of just one material: thin metal chains from a hardware store. The original interior of the former Prince Albert pub was left intact, with chains attached around the edge of each windowpane. The chains were then gathered together in bundles, slung from the ceiling, and hung above each of the tables in the restaurant, where they are arranged to form the flaring shades of the hanging lights. A total of sixty-eight miles (110 km) of chain is used.

Hotel Ballymun

Date **2007**

Place **Dublin, Ireland**

Designers **Seamus Nolan/various artists and designers**

Hotel Ballymun was a temporary hotel created within a condemned housing block in Ballymun in north Dublin, Ireland. The project, carried out by a group of artists and designers, was as much a creative statement as a functioning hotel, highlighting the wastefulness of tearing down buildings just a few decades after they were built, and exploring how unwanted dwellings could be given new life.

The suburb of Ballymun is infamous for the large-scale apartment blocks built according to the utopian architectural principles of the 1960s and 1970s, which are now widely considered a planning disaster. Like similar projects built in urban areas, the flats were intended to provide a better life for residents who had previously lived in poor situations in traditional housing. But conditions in the new complexes rapidly deteriorated, and the apartments soon came to symbolize poverty, alienation, and crime. Ballymun's apartments are now being replaced with new housing as part of a huge regeneration scheme.

Hotel Ballymun was established on the fifteenth floor of the Clarke Tower. It was open to the public for a month in the spring of 2007, with nine rooms created within the former apartments plus a sitting room, breakfast room, a conference room, and other facilities. The project was led by artist Seamus Nolan as part of Breaking Ground, an arts scheme funded by redevelopment company Ballymun Regeneration. Nolan worked with local people to convert the apartments into hotel rooms, which were cleaned and decorated but otherwise left in Spartan condition. The rooms, which offered spectacular views across Dublin, were furnished with one-off pieces made from salvaged furniture by local people in a series of workshops led by Irish design group Sticks and designer Jonathan Legge. A series of cultural events were held in the hotel while it was open, and at the end of the project the furnishings were auctioned to fund an arts bursary for Ballymun residents. The tower was demolished in 2007.

Barcode

Date **2006**

Place **London**

Designer **Woods Bagot Architects**

Located beneath railway arches in Vauxhall, London, Bar Code is a nightclub that attempts to be as environmentally friendly as possible. The arches are listed historical monuments, so they could not be altered during construction; therefore the club has been designed to touch the host structures as lightly as possible.

The designers, architectural firm Woods Bagot, have incorporated several features intended to reduce energy consumption, most notably the lighting system, which uses LEDs (light-emitting diodes) instead of incandescent bulbs. LEDs are more energy efficient—and hence cheaper to run—than traditional bulbs, and the designers claim the entire lighting system uses about the same amount of electricity as boiling water in an electric kettle. LEDs also give off practically no heat, meaning there is less need for artificial cooling systems in the club. The venue is naturally ventilated, although it does have an air-conditioning system as well, but the designers claim this is only needed on the hottest nights during the summer.

The LEDs are arranged in rows along the vaulted ceiling and behind translucent colored screens. Other electricity-saving tricks employed in the club include bar fridges that open from the top rather than from the front, which leads to less cold air escaping and hence to lower electricity consumption.

Nomad System

Date **2007**

Designers **Jaime Salm and Roger Allen/MIO**

Nomad System is a modular architectural system of recycled cardboard components that are slotted together to create interior screens, partitions, or even rooms without the need for tools and without damaging existing structures. The system is based on a single flat cardboard component that is die-cut with a series of slots and which has a shape rather like an old television screen. Two of these components slot together to form a cross, forming the basic building block of the system. The units can then be slotted together like a child's toy to create freestanding structures. By selecting different slots, either open or closed structures can be created.

Made from recycled kraft paper—a rough brown cardboard made from wood pulp that is widely used for grocery bags, envelopes, and packaging—the system is sold in packs of twenty-four units and comes in a range of colors. After their useful life, the modules can be recycled via normal neighborhood collection schemes. Nomad System is another example of the move towards more adaptable interior configurations that do not require structural work when changes are required. Cardboard is also a good insulation material, meaning that interior spaces created using products like Nomad System will retain warmth.

The product was designed by Jaime Salm and Roger Allen for MIO, a Philadelphia-based design brand that specializes in sustainable products. The company's products, which include furniture, wallpapers, lighting, and accessories, are all designed to minimize shipping, assembly, and disassembly requirements and to maximize reuse, recycling, and composting. MIO claims only to work with companies with socially responsible business practices.

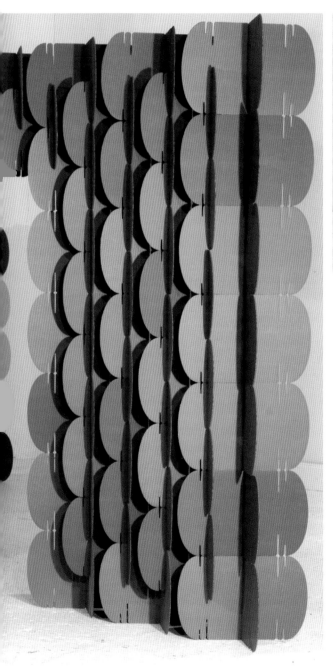

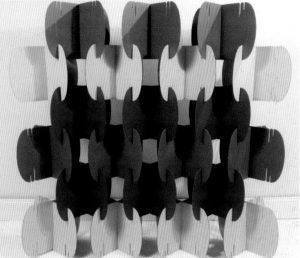

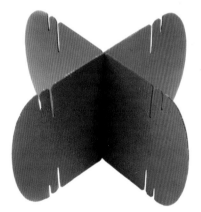

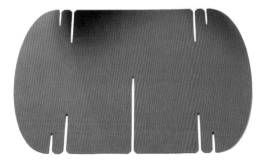

reHOUSE/BATH

Date **2007**
Place **Les Saintes-Maries-de-la-Mer, France**
Designers **Fulguro and Thomas Jomini Architecture**

This installation at the Château d'Avignon at Les Saintes-Maries-de-la-Mer in France was part of an ongoing series of investigations into domestic water conservation by Swiss design duo Fulguro. Called reHOUSE/BATH, the conceptual project suggests how the amount of water used to bathe could be dramatically reduced and the resulting gray water reused instead of being drained away. The user washes in a wide shallow bath, from which a network of tubes delivers waste water to pots containing houseplants.

The installation is a development of an earlier project called reHOUSE, which proposed a sustainable water network for a whole house that splits water into three types: drinking water, fresh water, and gray water. Planned as a thought-provoking exercise, reHOUSE was a collaboration between Fulguro, Swiss art and design school ECAL, and architect Thomas Jomini. Drinking water, piped in from the public water supply, is used only for drinking and cooking. Fresh water is collected from the roof and balcony and used for bathing, washing, and refrigeration (via water-fed, ceramic cooling models called hiberliths that operate on the same principle as Doshi Levien's Matlo watercooler on page 66). Gray water—runoff water from bathing and cooking—is first filtered and then used for cleaning and to water plants, which provide food. Organic waste from the toilets and kitchen are composted to provide food for the plants while biogas produced by the composting process is used as fuel for both ambient and water heating.

Fulguro have also designed a series of water-saving items that treat every drop of water as precious, including a plant pot that doubles as a stand for wet umbrellas and a metal rainwater collector in the shape of a large leaf that funnels rain into a plant pot.

Stitch Room

Date **2007**

Designers **Ronan and Erwan Bouroullec**

Stitch Room by French brothers Ronan and Erwan Bouroullec was created for an exhibition showcasing alternative interior concepts by leading designers, the My Home exhibition at the Vitra Design Museum in Weil am Rhein, Germany, in 2007. A system of informal shelters resembling shantytown dwellings and made of ecofriendly fabrics, it suggests a different kind of interior configuration, where internal spaces become more nomadic and relaxed. Stitch Room also allows existing interiors to be given new uses without wasteful demolition and rebuilding.

The structures are made up of modular panels of stiffened fabrics that snap together to form walls, ceilings, and floors. The panels, supported by lightweight aluminum poles that slip through the panels to form frames, create comfortable, warm, flexible zones within larger interior spaces.

The components can be customized and reused repeatedly, while the fabric panels provide thermal and acoustic insulation. The panels are made of environmentally friendly textiles produced by Danish brand Kvadrat. Kvadrat has a strong environmental ethic, banning the use of many harmful chemicals and having strict policies regarding the recycling of packaging and minimizing pollution.

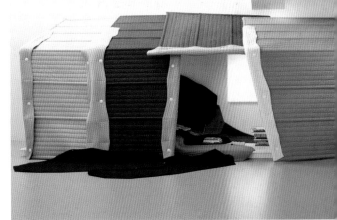

Subway Light Project

Date **2007**

Designer **Caroline Pham**

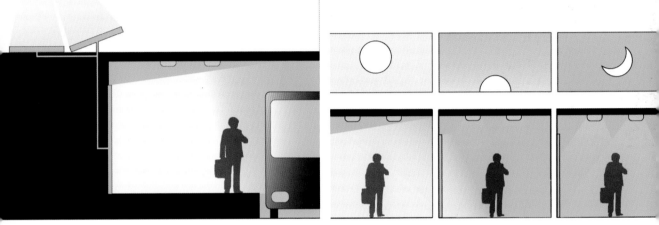

Subway Light Project is a conceptual study into how covered public spaces such as underpasses, subways, and car parks could be illuminated more efficiently and beautifully. Proposed by Caroline Pham, a student at Parsons the New School for Design in New York, the concept won first prize in the school's Sustainable Design Review in 2007. The project employs a technology called "sunlight transportation," which collects sunlight and channels it down fiber-optic cables to illuminate interior spaces. Pham's proposal, which has so far not been realized, is to use the technology to illuminate large public art panels in otherwise dark, gloomy spaces.

Sunlight transportation systems collect sunlight via mirrored dishes mounted on rooftops that track the sun during the day, channeling sunlight down bundles of fiber-optic cables that act like light pipes. The collectors filter out the dangerous ultraviolet and heat-causing infrared spectrums, meaning the light fibers are cool enough to touch. The cables feed into lighting diffusing units located in ceilings, or in this case on a wall. Each unit can produce enough

light to illuminate around 1,000 square feet (93 sq m) of space. On bright days, the systems can provide up to 80 percent of a building's lighting requirements and are 50 percent efficient, meaning half the sunlight they collect is fed into the lighting units. This compares to the estimated 15 percent efficiency of photovoltaic cells, which convert sunlight into electricity that must then be converted back into light.

An estimated 30 percent of all energy consumed is used to light buildings. Sunlight transportation systems could help reduce energy consumption, although they are limited by the relatively short distance—30–50 feet (9–15 m)—that the fiber-optic cables can carry light before losing brightness. In addition, the technology only works optimally when the sun is shining, losing effectiveness on cloudy days. A related technology called "hybrid solar lighting" solves these problems by integrating sunlight transportation systems with incandescent or fluorescent lights, which are computer-controlled to come on when natural lighting levels are low.

Boekhandel Selexyz Dominicanen

Date **2007**
Place **Maastricht, Netherlands**
Designer **Merkx + Girod Architects**

This bookshop, created inside a disused Dominican church in Maastricht in the Netherlands, is an example of how existing but unwanted buildings can be adapted to new uses without having to knock them down and replace them with a new structure. The idea has clear environmental advantages, since a lot of energy is used when constructing a new building. The total amount of energy used to extract and prepare raw materials, transport them, and assemble them is called the "embodied energy" of a building, and this can amount to as much as 25 percent of the total energy requirements of a building over its lifetime. It is therefore beneficial to extend the useful life of a structure as much as possible, because demolition and reconstruction waste vast amounts of energy and resources.

Since Napoleonic occupation ended its use as a religious building in the late eighteenth century, the eight-hundred-year-old Maastricht church has been used variously as a warehouse, a market, a beer hall, and, most recently, a bicycle park. In 2007 it was assigned yet another new use, as a branch of Dutch bookshop chain Selexyz. The narrow nave and aisles, interrupted with huge columns, did not leave much space for a traditional bookshop layout, so architects Merkx + Girod stacked the bookshop vertically on a multilevel steel structure that is akin to a giant bookshelf. Gantries allow customers to browse books on the upper levels.

The building's services, such as heating and cooling, are stored in the crypt, keeping the lofty interior of the church as clear as possible. Every element of the bookshop has been designed to do as little damage to the structure of the church as possible, ensuring that, at some point in the future, everything can be removed and the church reused for yet another purpose.

The Catch

Date **2007**
Designer **Julia Lohmann**

This temporary installation, as much an artwork as a piece of design, makes a statement about overfishing. It was created by German designer Julia Lohmann while on a three-month residency in Sapporo, Japan, and was inspired by a visit to the giant Tsukiji fish market in Tokyo, where 4.4 million pounds (2 million kg) of fish are sold each day.

The Catch features a room full of empty wooden fish boxes taken from Sapporo's fish market and joined together to form a large breaking wave that is 106 inches (270 cm) high. This wave of timber represents an empty, lifeless ocean. At the center of the installation is a small circular room constructed of upended fish roe boxes. The room is bare and is meant to resemble a chapel that has been stripped of its contents by raiders. The room is lit by candles in holders made of tuna vertebrae, which are placed in the fish-box niches like votive candles in a temple.

Japan is the world's largest consumer of fish and has the world's largest fishing fleet. Global demand for fish and seafood is pushing many species to the brink of collapse. Oceans cover over three-quarters of the planet and contain 80 percent of all life on earth, yet recent studies suggest that one-third of all fishing stocks worldwide have collapsed to less than 10 percent of former levels, and that if current fishing levels continue, all fish stocks worldwide could collapse within fifty years.

The layout of the Catch is based on the Almadraba—a maze of fishing nets, called *raveras*, traditionally used in Andalucia, Spain, to catch shoals of migrating tuna in a central pool called a *copo*. The technique is now becoming obsolete due to the depletion of tuna stocks.

The Ethical Kitchen

Date **2007**

Designer **Alexandra Sten Jørgensen**

Kitchens are the source of much waste, in terms of uneaten food that is thrown away; water that is used carelessly; power and fuel consumed by stoves, refrigerators, and other gadgets; and food packaging and other materials that are thrown away.

Alexandra Sten Jørgensen is one of several designers exploring ways of reducing waste in the kitchen. Her Ethical Kitchen, designed while a student at Buckinghamshire New University in the U.K., is a conceptual project that uses wastewater and food to feed climbing plants, which are trained over the kitchen units. Organic waste is composted in an integrated bin, and gray water from washing vegetables is recycled to water the plants. Drawers beneath the counter are for temporary storage of packaging for recycling. The effectiveness of the user's recycling is apparent: if the plant is not fed, it will die.

The project has much in common with reHOUSE/BATH by Fulguro and Thomas Jomini (see page 188), which uses bathwater to sustain houseplants. Dutch designer John Arndt has created a similar project, the Kitchen of Terrestrial Mechanics, which uses water dripping from an overhead dish rack to water herbs. Dripping water is also used to cool food stored in unglazed ceramic containers in Arndt's project.

Green kitchen concepts appear to be catching on. In 2008, consumer appliance brand Whirlpool showcased GreenKitchen. Resembling a modern fitted kitchen, GreenKitchen shares some of the approaches of Sten Jørgensen and Arndt but through technological means. The cold water that runs when a hot tap is first turned on is diverted to water plants kept in an integrated greenhouse-like compartment. Heat generated by the fridge's compressor motor is used to heat water for the dishwasher. A low-energy cool space keeps vegetables and other foods at cellar temperature, requiring less energy than a fridge. Combined with other low-energy appliances, Whirlpool estimates the design could reduce energy consumption by half.

The Farm Project

Date **2006**

Designers **Mike Meiré/Dornbracht**

Created as a mobile exhibition for kitchen manufacturer Dornbracht by German designer Mike Meiré, the Farm Project is an attempt to move kitchen design away from the minimalist aesthetic that dominates today. Instead, it proposes a return to the working methods and appearance of a traditional farmhouse kitchen, complete with live animals, herbs growing in pots, and a table that serves both for food preparation and dining.

Meiré's intention was to reestablish the connection between the food we eat and where it comes from—a connection that has been broken by the rise of supermarkets and preprepared, overpackaged ingredients. The Farm Project instead presents an idealized kitchen where many of the ingredients are found just outside the door in the farmyard or fields, or even in the kitchen itself, since the installation features a pen full of live pigs and goats, cages of live chickens and ducks, and tanks of fish.

The kitchen is housed in a demountable structure akin to that of a greenhouse, but which is clad in panels of various materials such as timber and laminate instead of glass. Every spare inch of the interior is used for storage or display, with pots, pans, and cured hams slung from the ceiling, utensils hanging on the walls, and ingredients and crockery stacked on tall open shelves.

First presented in Milan in 2006 during the city's international furniture fair, the Farm Project was later shown at design fairs in Cologne and Miami. At these events, cooks prepared snacks and meals that were served to visitors to prove that it was a working kitchen rather than just a showroom.

Apart from the enveloping structure, the kitchen has not really been designed at all, and has instead been assembled by kitchen staff according to their needs, under the art direction of Meiré. The point here is that design often comes between people and real, sensual experiences, and serves to distance us from the realities behind certain aspects of food production such as the slaughter of animals.

Sayama Flats

Date **2008**

Place **Sayama, Tokyo, Japan**

Designers **Jo Nagasaka/Schemata Architecture Office**

Sayama Flats by Schemata Architecture Office is an example of how an existing building—in this case an apartment block—can undergo a major refurbishment without stripping out, discarding, and replacing every element of the building. Sayama Flats is a renovation project of a twenty-nine-year-old apartment building in Sayama, a residential suburb about an hour by train from central Tokyo. The renovation project, completed in January 2008, was designed by Jo Nagasaka of Schemata Architecture Office in Tokyo, who have turned the unremarkable seven-story block into a kind of residential laboratory where the mostly young inhabitants are encouraged to develop their own lifestyles.

In Japan, old buildings are often simply demolished and replaced, or at least stripped back to their cores and completely rebuilt around the original superstructure. Reusing the core of a building in this way can save resources and avoid putting large amounts of concrete and other materials into landfills. Schemata Architecture Office has removed many of the building's internal features, leaving the concrete columns, walls, and ceilings visible and revealing services such as water pipes and electricity ducting. Most of the flimsy partitions dividing the flats into rooms have also been removed, creating large, flexible spaces that residents have customized with lightweight dividing solutions such as curtains and freestanding dividers. Many of the building's young residents have furnished their flats with found objects or thrift-store purchases.

Other original elements, however, have been left in place, where they still function and do not need replacing, including many of the kitchens and bathrooms. These remain in the flats, their diverse styles serving as reminders of the previous occupants of the building.

Vertical Gardens

Date **2007**
Designer **Patrick Blanc**

Vertical gardens have become almost de rigueur in avant-garde architectural projects recently, with architects including Jean Nouvel, MVRDV, Herzog & de Meuron, and SANAA integrating spectacular walls of living plants into their buildings. Nouvel's Musée du Quai Branly in Paris features an entire office building clad in plants, while MVRDV's Gyre shopping mall in Tokyo has an indoor wall that is completely smothered in foliage. All are the work of one man, French botanist Patrick Blanc, a trained scientist who is also a researcher at the French National Center for Scientific Research in Paris and the author of many books on plant life.

Over the years, Blanc has perfected a way of growing plants against a vertical wall without the need for soil. When mature, his installations resemble verdant jungles and are used on interior and exterior walls, both for the beauty of the plants themselves and to improve the environment via the plants' ability to absorb airborne pollutants. The gardens also act as effective sound and heat insulators.

During his botanical expeditions around the world, Blanc observed that plants often grew on vertical surfaces such as rock faces, walls, or tree trunks without soil if there was a constant supply of water. His Vertical Gardens replicate this phenomenon artificially. The gardens start with a metal frame that is fixed to the wall and then covered in 0.04-inch-thick (1 mm) PVC sheeting to keep the wall dry. A sheet of rot-proof polyamide felt is attached on top to absorb water and distribute it across the surface of the wall via capillary action, ensuring that plants inserted into pockets cut into the felt are irrigated. As long as they receive an uninterrupted flow of water, plants do not require soil and will not produce roots that burrow into the wall and damage it. Instead, roots spread harmlessly across the surface of the wall.

Vertical Gardens require an irrigation system and the water needs to be nutrient-rich, but apart from that they are self-sustaining (although indoor gardens require artificial lighting) and last for many years without intervention.

Architecture

Architects have been showing concern for the environment longer than designers in other fields, and as buildings are the most resource-hungry field of human activity, they have the greatest potential role to play in promoting less-wasteful design practices. Leading contemporary figures including Norman Foster, Richard Rogers, and Renzo Piano have been promoting energy-efficient architecture for years, viewing features such as passive ventilation, photovoltaics, and intelligent solar orientation to minimize overheating as natural extensions of their desire to create buildings that are as efficient and pleasurable as possible.

However, architects have to deal with clients who are often reluctant to adopt greener building practices if these mean spending more on their buildings. As a result, green features often get squeezed out of commercial schemes late in the design stage in order to save money, even though spending just 1 percent extra at the time of construction can lead to energy efficiencies of up to 30 percent throughout the life of the building.

Green architecture is not just about reducing the energy consumption of the finished building. Green building codes highlight the need to minimize environmental damage to the site and the surrounding area; to reduce water consumption; to promote the use of recycled and recyclable building materials; and to ensure buildings provide a healthy indoor environment.

The examples shown in this chapter—a mix of completed projects and as-yet unbuilt proposals—have been selected

to show the diversity of ways that architects are meeting environmental challenges: from small-scale low-tech approaches such as DesignBuildBLUFF's Rosie Joe House in Utah, built of cheap or salvaged local materials by members of the local community, to sophisticated, high-tech structures such as Behnisch, Behnisch & Partner's Norddeutsche Landesbank in Hanover, Germany.

Despite this diversity of approaches, there seems to be a tendency for leading architects to once again explore vernacular solutions that worked in the past but which were forgotten during the twentieth century's obsession with industrial, artificial solutions. Foster + Partners' Masdar Initiative is perhaps the most striking example of this trend. The vast town close to Abu Dhabi in the United Arab Emirates is being billed as "the world's first zero-carbon, zero-energy city," yet it appears closely modeled on ancient Arabian walled cities.

Finally, the huge pressures caused by rapid urbanization in the developing world and the predicted rise in climate change–induced natural disasters look set to create problems on a hitherto unprecedented scale for architects and planners. The Make It Right project in New Orleans is a small example of the kind of thinking that will be required in the future to provide shelter for the less fortunate in a rapidly changing world.

9 Stock Orchard Street

Date **2004**

Place **London**

Designers **Sarah Wigglesworth and Jeremy Till/Sarah Wigglesworth Architects**

Officially called 9 Stock Orchard Street after its address, but better known as the Straw Bale House, this combined home and office in London is one of the most celebrated examples of sustainable design in the U.K. It was built by Sarah Wigglesworth and Jeremy Till for use as both a family home and an office for their architectural practice. The house, built on a patch of land overlooking a railroad line, incorporates dozens of different approaches to sustainability and is akin to an experimental laboratory for green materials and ideas.

By putting their home and office in the same building, the couple have eliminated the need to commute. Architecturally and technically, the house eschews high-tech systems and instead adopts earthy, informal solutions. Materials are chosen to reduce environmental impact, and with its willow-hurdle gate, its mini meadow, its undercroft complete with chickens, and its wild-strawberry roof garden, the house is like an eccentric farmhouse in the middle of the city. Its nickname comes from the straw bales used as insulation in the north-facing wall. The bales, which have very low embodied energy, are recyclable, cheap, and provide extremely high levels of insulation. The bale wall wraps around the bedroom area, keeping it warm.

The building is raised on pillars of broken reclaimed concrete blocks inside wire cages like the gabions used on roadsides—although due to building regulations they are not structural and contain steel columns. These have very little embodied energy and were constructed on-site. The ground around the building is planted as a meadow and is unpaved, to aid natural drainage. Pitch-pine railroad ties found on the site are recycled for window frames, while the wall facing the railroad is made of sandbags filled with concrete to insulate the house both thermally and acoustically.

Inside, the home features a brick "beehive" pantry, built in the shape of an African hut to keep the interior cool while heat escapes through a hole at the top. Rainwater is collected from the roof in large barrels that supply a composting toilet, while photovoltaics power the underfloor heating and solar panels heat the water. The house is so well insulated that the wood-burning stove in the living area is only required during the coldest six weeks of the year.

The Micro-Compact Home

Date **2005**

Place **Munich, Germany**

Architects **Horden Cherry Lee/Haack + Höpfner**

More akin to a luxury trailer than a house, the Micro-Compact Home is a lightweight, low-energy, compact dwelling for one or two people. By stripping away nonessential items and squeezing living space, storage, and services into an aluminum-clad 8-foot, 4-inch (2.65 m), 2-ton (1.8 tonne) cube, designer Richard Horden of Horden Cherry Lee Architects and his assistant Lydia Haack have created a home that forces the user to focus on essentials and live a less materialistic life.

The Micro-Compact Home, or m-ch as it is known, is designed primarily for business or leisure use, although the manufacturers claim it is suitable for longer-term living. Each unit contains spaces and equipment for sleeping, working, dining, cooking, and washing, with two double beds, a slide-out dining table that can seat up to five, a kitchen area, and a shower and toilet cubicle.

The m-ch was inspired by business-class air travel, and many of its features are derived from the aviation and automotive industries rather than the housebuilding sector. Each unit features air-conditioning, warm-air heating, a flat-screen television, plus fire alarms and smoke detectors.

The units require an electrical supply and water, but apart from that they can be located anywhere, as they are designed to make minimal impact on the ground. They consist of a subframe with three legs, which raises the dwelling above the ground, thus providing natural space and airflow between the cube and the ground. The legs are height-adjustable to enable the homes to be located horizontally on any gradient. Their size means that in many parts of the world, planning permission is not required. The small interior space can be heated and cooled efficiently, and a low-energy version of the home, with photovoltaic cells and a wind generator, is also available.

Up to five Micro-Compact Homes can be delivered on the back of a trailer truck and they are light enough to be lifted into place by crane or, in exceptional circumstances, a helicopter. At the end of their life, the manufacturers offer to collect and recycle the units.

Chimney Pot Park

Date **2007**

Place **Salford, England**

Designers **Urban Splash/Shed KM Architects**

Chimney Pot Park is an attempt to repopulate a blighted urban area without totally demolishing it and starting again. The project involved redeveloping ten blocks of small two-bedroom family townhomes built in 1910 for industrial workers at Seedley and Langworthy in Salford, Greater Manchester, England. This formerly vibrant district had become a no-go zone, with the lack of industrial employment and crime driving out the original inhabitants. Because there were no willing takers of the old-fashioned homes, most of them were boarded up and slated for demolition.

Manchester-based property developer Urban Splash made its name in the 1990s by converting unwanted inner-city industrial buildings into desirable loft-style apartments, finding new uses for beautiful old premises that would otherwise have been knocked down and, in the process, making city-center living fashionable again. Like many other cities around the world, central Manchester had witnessed rapid depopulation during the second half of the twentieth century as industries closed down and the middle classes moved to sprawling suburban housing developments—an urban model that is regarded as highly unsustainable due to the dependence on cars and the inefficient use of land.

Chimney Pot Park was Urban Splash's first attempt at tackling blighted row housing, and its solution was to leave the streets and the street-facing brick façades intact while totally rebuilding the rest of the houses. Inside, the houses have been turned upside down, with bedrooms on the ground floor and living areas upstairs. The small backyards have been replaced by a raised, shared terrace garden extending the length of the street, with a secure parking lot beneath. The distinctive chimneystacks that gave the area its nickname have been replaced with protruding roof lights that approximate the chimneys while bringing daylight into the homes.

While this project may not be as laden with ecological features as other schemes, it nonetheless is a pioneering attempt to create socially sustainable neighborhoods in urban areas without the need for wholesale—and often misguided—rebuilding.

Rincon Mountain Residence

Date **2006**

Place **Tuscon, Arizona**

Designer **DesignBuild Collaborative**

Rammed-earth construction is an ancient building method that is finding new favor in environmentally friendly building projects. The technique has been used for centuries in areas where timber or stone is scarce or transportation is difficult, as load-bearing walls can be made from earth found at the construction site. Rammed earth helps reduce the need for heating or cooling systems as its high thermal mass allows it to store heat during the day and release heat at night, helping to regulate temperatures inside. This makes it a particularly suitable material for buildings in extreme climates such as deserts.

Architects DesignBuild Collaborative of Tucson, Arizona, have used rammed earth in several of their projects, including this rammed-earth and scoria house called Rincon Mountain Residence in a remote mountainous area east of Tuscon. The home is designed to function completely "off-grid," with electricity generated by photovoltaic panels and a hydrogen fuel cell. Apart from rammed earth, the residence is constructed of steel, timber, and local stone, and internal walls are lined with scoria, a lightweight, insulating material made of volcanic rock. To create the building's walls, moistened local earth was mixed with a small amount of Portland cement and packed between timber formwork erected on-site. The earth was added to a depth of a few inches at a time and then "tamped" (packed down) to compact it. Originally done by hand with sticks, tamping is done mechanically today. Once the earth has filled to the top of the formwork, the timber is removed, leaving the solid earth wall behind. Usually the surface of the wall is then sealed to protect it from the elements. Correctly built rammed earth walls can last indefinitely—even in wetter climates—and the addition of cement, as with this project, increases their load-bearing capacity.

Rammed earth construction is similar to adobe, one of the earliest of all building methods and one that is also used today by DesignBuild Collaborative. Adobe, which has been used in the Southwest for thousands of years, involves making bricks of damp earth mixed with dung or straw and then dried in the sun.

Rosie Joe House

Date **2004**
Place **Bluff, Utah**
Designer **DesignBuildBLUFF**

Located in the small rural town of Bluff in Utah's San Juan River Valley, the Rosie Joe House is an exercise in self-sufficiency. It was built in 2004 for Rosie Joe, a single Navajo working mother, by a group of eight architecture students from the DesignBuildBLUFF program at the University of Utah's College of Architecture and Planning. The program promotes an approach to architecture that is rooted in community and environmental concerns, with students acting as both designers and builders and immersing themselves in the culture of the people who will use the finished buildings.

The Rosie Joe House reflects the lack of amenities available to the Navajo community in Bluff, using cheap or salvaged construction materials where possible and functioning "off grid." Its defining feature is the crinkly tin butterfly roof that is raised clear of the dwelling on a framework of welded rebar (a reinforcing steel bar). The roof, which is larger in surface area than the living areas beneath, is designed both to catch rain and channel it into a large storage tank and to shade the house.

The home also features an 18-inch-thick (46 cm) thick rammed-earth, sun-facing "trombe" wall made from sand and clay that was dug and sifted on site. Rammed-earth walls are extremely good at regulating temperatures in extreme climates, reducing the need for air-conditioning during the day or heating at night. The south-facing wall is made of found windows in a variety of materials, and the timber ceiling is made entirely of recycled pallets. Exterior walls are made of straw—an extremely cheap and highly insulating material—sandwiched between sheets of clear acrylic, while the interior walls are clad with discarded road signs.

The DesignBuildBLUFF program is based on the principles established by the late architect Samuel Mockbee at the Rural Studio project in Alabama, which promotes architectural solutions that come from within communities rather than being imported from elsewhere.

BedZED

Date **2002**

Place **Sutton, England**

Designer **Bill Dunster**

Beddington Zero Energy Development, or BedZED for short, is a carbon-neutral housing project that aims to generate as much energy as it consumes. It does this both by reducing energy needs to a minimum and producing the power it does require from renewable resources on-site. Designed by British architect Bill Dunster for London housing charity the Peabody Trust, the development consists of eighty-two houses and seventeen apartments near Wallington in the borough of Sutton, southeast London.

Most of the green techniques used on the development are low-tech. The highly insulated homes are arranged in south-facing terraces, with large triple-glazed windows to retain the warming effect of the sun and reduce artificial lighting requirements during the day. A survey in 2003 found that space-heating requirements were 88 percent less than the U.K. norm. The buildings are built wherever possible from natural, recycled, or reclaimed materials, and efforts were made to source most of the raw materials from within 35 miles (56 km) to reduce transportation. Rainwater from the roofs is collected and reused. Power comes from an on-site combined heat and power (CHP) plant that generates both electricity and heat, which is used to warm the buildings. The plant is fueled by timber offcuts from the tree-surgery industry that would otherwise be dumped. This type of fuel is regarded as carbon neutral since burning the timber releases the same amount of carbon as the wood absorbed while it was growing. Photovoltaic panels also generate electricity.

BedZED aims to reduce residents' car use by 50 percent compared to a normal housing development. The site contains office space, a nursery, and a community center, giving residents the opportunity to work and meet without leaving the development, while a car-sharing scheme and limited parking spaces are designed to minimize car ownership. To encourage walking, BedZED is designed around "home zone" principles, with road layouts that keep vehicles to walking pace and pedestrian-friendly features such as good lighting and low curbs for strollers and wheelchair users.

Accordion House

Date **2004**
Place **Varmland, Sweden**
Designer **24H Architecture**

The rustic lakeside summerhouse is a key lifestyle accessory for many urban Swedes, who like to get back to nature in both summer and winter. Many have no electricity, running water, or other services, and the cabins generally have a minimal environmental impact. In order to preserve its pristine wilderness areas from overdevelopment, Sweden has strict environmental laws banning construction of new huts and severely limiting the amount of extension work that can be done on existing ones. So when Maartje Lammers and Boris Zeisser of Rotterdam-based architects 24H Architecture sought a rural family retreat in Sweden—where Zeisser had spent his summers as a youth—they had to think creatively.

They bought a tiny, dilapidated fisherman's cabin dating from the 1800s on the shore of Lake Övre Gla in the Glaskogen nature reserve in Varmland and set about restoring and extending it. Since regulations ban extensions larger than the original building, and because the extreme Swedish winter makes a large drafty cabin unappealing, they came up with a novel solution: the cantilevered, glazed extension slides in and out of the original hut to create a large living space in summer and a cosy double-insulated nest in winter. The extension moves on bearings along steel rails using a manual pulley system, cantilevering out over a stream.

Named *Dragspelhuset* and dubbed the Accordion House by neighbors, both hut and extension are clad in *stickor*—the Swedish term for traditional timber shingles. However, the shingles are actually made from imported Canadian cedar, which lasts much longer than local timbers and requires no maintenance. The hut has additional green features, including solar-powered lights, and the walls of the extension are lined with highly insulating reindeer hides—a technique traditionally employed by the indigenous Sámi people of Scandinavia.

The Accordion House, as in the work of Terunobu Fujimori (see page 216), explores how vernacular building techniques and folkloric architectural mannerisms can be adopted to contemporary needs.

Teahouse on Stilts

Date **2004**
Place **Chino, Nagano, Japan**
Designer **Terunobu Fujimori**

The work of Japanese architect Terunobu Fujimori explores the relationship between the natural and the manmade, which he believes is one of the key issues facing civilization in the twenty-first century. His buildings, which often incorporate living plants or trees, attempt to find aesthetic—rather than technical—harmony between their manmade forms and the landscapes in which they are sited. Relatively low-tech in their construction, their structures are usually built of steel, mortar, and plywood. The exteriors employ natural materials such as timber, stone, and earth; interiors often feature handworked natural materials such as grass and reeds. Then come the plants: the roof of his Chive House is covered with hundreds of pots of chives; Dandelion House (see page 218, top, and 219) features dandelion plants growing between timber slats on the façade and roof; and Single Pine House (see page 218, bottom left and right) has a pine tree growing on top of its pyramid-shaped roof. Plants are integrated into the buildings—rather than used in separate landscaping schemes—as a reaction against the way that landscaping and architecture are usually considered to be separate entities on contemporary projects.

Teahouse on Stilts (called *Takasugi-an,* shown on this and facing pages) is Fujimori's smallest project in a portfolio that includes private houses and a university building, yet it represents his unusual architectural style. Designed for his own use in his home village in the hills of Chino in Nagano Prefecture, it features plywood walls and a hand-beaten copper roof. The structure's Japanese name means "an overly tall hermitage."

Fujimori, a professor of architecture at the University of Tokyo, has also proposed a future city concept that is radically different from most architects' high-tech visions of the future. Tokyo Plan 2101, a conceptual project presented at the Venice Architecture Biennale in 2006, imagines that many of today's urban areas will be abandoned as sea levels rise due to global warming. Fujimori proposed new cities made of coral and wood, both materials that he says store large amounts of carbon. This would ensure that the carbon they contain would remain locked in the building rather than being released into the atmosphere.

Skive CHP Station

Date **2006**

Place **Skive, Denmark**

Designer **CF Møller Architects**

Located beside a fjord close to the town of Skive in Denmark, this power station is notable not only for its architecture but for the way it generates both electricity and heat for local homes from plant matter. Whereas a traditional power station generates only electricity, a combined heat and power (CHP, or cogeneration) plant captures the heat produced as a by-product of the generating process and which would otherwise be wasted. The captured heat, in the form of hot water, can be pumped through pipes to heat local homes and businesses. Popular in Scandinavia, CHP is far more efficient than generating electricity and heat separately.

The Skive plant is doubly innovative since it runs on biomass rather than fossil fuels. Biomass is harvested or recycled biological material such as wood, straw, and vegetable oil that can be burned as a fuel. As long as the material is harvested in a sustainable way, biomass is theoretically a carbon-neutral fuel source because the carbon absorbed by the plants during their lives is released back into the atmosphere when they are burned. However, when the fossil fuels used to grow and transport the crops are taken into account, there is an inevitable net output of carbon. Skive uses a process called biomass gasification, which first turns the organic matter into gas by subjecting it to extremely high temperatures while adding oxygen. The resulting gas burns more efficiently than the biomass itself, and therefore generates more electricity and heat.

The Skive CHP Station is the largest biomass gasification plant in the world. It was designed by Danish architects CF Møller, who have turned a potential eyesore on this flat stretch of coast into a striking architectural landmark. The main part of the plant is clad in copper panels, which will patinate over time, turning green. The plant's two chimneys are made of Corten, a type of prerusted steel.

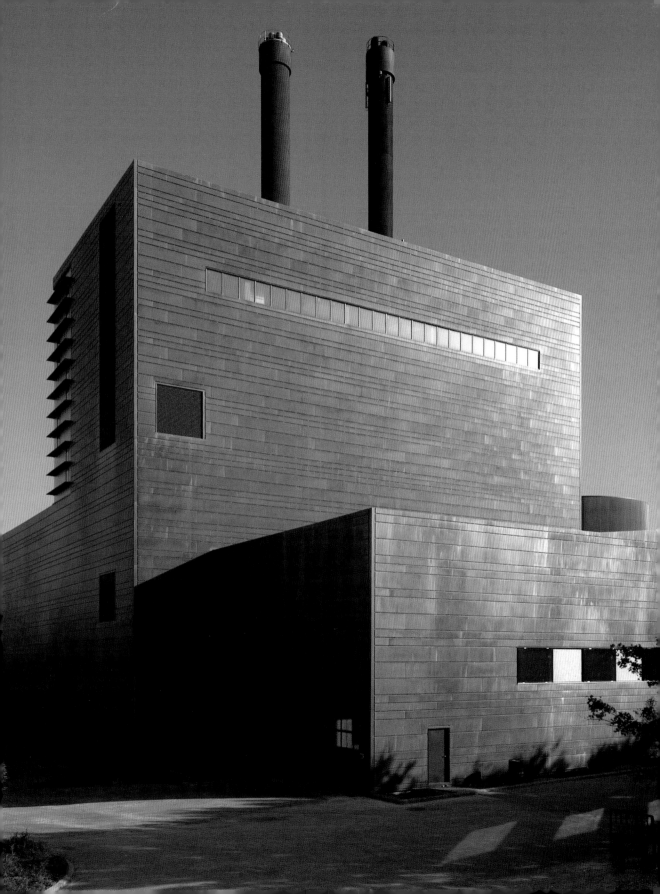

Make It Right

Date **2006**

Place **New Orleans**

Designers **Various architects**

Hurricane Katrina was the worst natural disaster ever to hit the United States, leaving more than 1,800 dead and causing an estimated $80 billion in damage in August 2005.

The city of New Orleans suffered the worst damage and greatest loss of life when rising floodwaters caused the protective system of raised levees to fail catastrophically. Much of the city, including many of its poorest districts, were inundated, including the vibrant Lower Ninth Ward, renowned for its cultural mix and musical traditions, as well as its architecture of porches and stoops. Although disadvantaged, this part of the city had a high percentage of home ownership, meaning the community was more stable than in other districts.

The Make It Right (MIR) project was launched in December 2006 by film star Brad Pitt, with the intention of ensuring that rebuilding work in the city was both sustainable and affordable to residents who had lost their homes. The project aims to build 150 new homes in the Lower Ninth Ward while developing a system that could be replicated elsewhere. With Pitt's celebrity power, leading architects from around the world were invited to design homes that would give the district the architectural character it had enjoyed before the devastation, but that would be better equipped to withstand any future floods.

Architects originally assigned to the project include American practice Morphosis, British architect David Adjaye, MVRDV of the Netherlands, and Shigeru Ban of Japan. The project aims to ensure that the former architectural character of the area informs the new designs, and participating architects were briefed on the area's vernacular traditions, such as the Shotgun, the Camelback, and the Creole Cottage housing styles.

Make It Right is a nonprofit organization that is now raising funds to build the homes, each of which is projected to cost around $150,000.

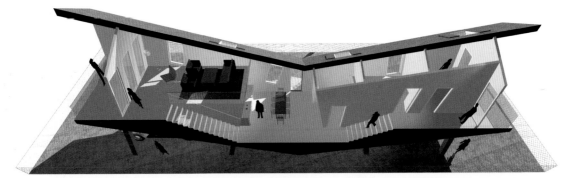

Dutch Pavilion

Date **2000**

Place **Hanover, Germany**

Designer **MVRDV**

As the earth's population grows, so more and more of the planet's virgin habitats are being cleared for agriculture. In response, the concept of the "vertical farm" has emerged as a theoretical way of taking the pressure off the countryside by stacking growing crops and livestock in tall buildings close to the cities where the food products they produce are required. Dutch Pavilion by architects MVRDV is a prototype of this concept that was built as the Dutch contribution to Expo 2000 in Hanover, Germany.

The temporary project consists of a number of different, typically Dutch landscapes stacked one above the other in an open-sided tower and connected by a staircase that winds its way around the edge of the entire structure. Visitors begin their journey on the upper level, which is called the Windmill floor and on which are mounted three slender wind turbines that generate the building's power while a landscaped pond collects rainwater.

Below this is the Rain floor, where water from the pond above cascades down and is purified. Underneath is the Forest floor, a triple-height level planted with oak trees nurtured by water from the level above. This level suggests how threatened natural landscapes such as forests could be recreated as public parks within tall buildings. Next is the Pots level. Here, the giant pots that contain the trees on the level above can be seen suspended from the ceiling, reinforcing the artificiality of the forest. These double as screens for displaying information, while other pots contain toilets and storage.

The Green House level contains thousands of flowering plants growing under artificial light, representing the Dutch flower industry, while below this the subterranean Dunes level consists of an eerie artificial landscape of undulating concrete. This level expresses the infertility of the band of sand dunes that protects the Netherlands from the sea. MVRDV has also proposed a more radical version of this concept: a skyscraper for livestock called Pigcity. Such buildings could be built in large numbers, allowing vast areas of farmland to be returned to nature or given over to leisure use.

Reichstag

Date **1999**
Place **Berlin**
Designer **Foster + Partners**

On its completion in 1999, the Reichstag parliament building in Berlin became an instant symbol both of newly reunified Germany and of sustainable design. The building's design united a commitment to democracy and transparency with a declaration of Germany's environmental aspirations, making clear in built form the nation's deep commitment to a green agenda. One of the more progressive nations when it comes to developing clean industries, Germany has invested heavily in wind power, and renewable power provides around 13 percent of the nation's electricity needs. A generous subsidy system encourages households and businesses to install equipment such as wind turbines and photovoltaic panels to generate power.

Designed by British architects Foster + Partners, the Reichstag is a major refurbishment of an existing building rather than a new build. An example of a structure that has proved adaptable to changing needs, it was built in 1894 to house the first German parliament and was in use until 1933, when it was severely damaged by fire. After a period of disuse it was refurbished in the 1960s and in 1990 selected as the parliamentary home of post-reuinification Germany.

Foster has retained the thick stone façade, which acts as an effective heat sink, keeping the building warm in winter and cool in summer. The building has its own "cogenerator" or combined heat and power (CHP) plant that runs on vegetable oil. In its first years the plant was augmented by power from coal and nuclear power stations, but in 2008 parliament agreed to source all power from renewable sources. Surplus heat is stored in an aquifer 984 feet (300 m) below ground, from where it can be pumped to heat the building when required.

The dramatic glass cupola that surmounts the debating chamber is both a symbol of democracy—the public can climb a helical ramp to the top of the dome and look down on elected representatives—and a device that funnels daylight into the building via a series of mirrors.

Flower Tower

Date **2004**
Place **Paris**
Designer **Edouard François**

This ten-story apartment block in the northwest of Paris uses living plants as a climate-control system. Designed by French architect Edouard François, the Flower Tower is sheathed in bamboo plants that grow in pots set along each of the narrow cantilevered balconies running around each floor. He was inspired by the way Parisians cultivate plants on even the tiniest balconies, adding beauty and pleasure to the city. Besides giving residents the sense of being surrounded by gardens, the plants diffuse heat, light, and wind, shading and screening the apartments. There are 380 cast-concrete pots on Flower Tower in total, all irrigated automatically by a network of hoses built into the balustrade.

François is emerging as one of the most interesting green-leaning architects. Flower Tower builds on one of his earlier projects, Holiday Homes in Jupilles. These rustic rural lodges, built on the edge of a national park, feature external walls lined with growing trees, which are trained to spread along the walls to create a jacket of leaves that makes the lodges almost invisible.

Before Flower Tower, François was best known for another plant-covered project, his Château-le-Lez housing project in the Antigone district of Montpellier in France. Built for a private-property developer and completed in 2000, the arcing sixty-four-apartment block has a façade that resembles a rock face. It is constructed of gabions—steel cages filled with rocks—that also contain soil and seeds so that over time the entire building will become overgrown with plants. The project, which has been nicknamed "the sprouting building," is also distinctive for its large timber-fenced balconies, some of which cantilever from the façade, and others of which are supported on steel legs.

10 X 10 Housing Project

Date **2007**

Place **Cape Town, South Africa**

Designers **Various architects and designers**

Many cities in the developing world are suffering acute shortages of decent housing as people abandon rural poverty in search of a better life in urban areas. This process of mass urbanization often happens spontaneously, resulting in vast informal settlements, or slums, on peripheral land around and within cities.

Cape Town in South Africa is one such city, where an estimated three million people live in shacks constructed of salvaged materials. Government resettlement programs are hampered by a lack of funds and the sheer numbers of new economic migrants who arrive each year from other parts of South Africa and neighboring countries.

The 10 x 10 Housing Project is an attempt to pioneer new, affordable housing types that are suitable for conditions in South Africa and other developing-world countries. Established in 2007 by Cape Town design-conference and exhibition company Design Indaba, the project paired ten international architects and designers with ten local firms. A central requirement of the brief was that each 430-square-foot (40 sq m) family home had to cost no more than just $6,200, the amount allocated by the government for state housing projects. All the designers gave their time for free and Design Indaba intends to make blueprints, specifications, and cost information freely available once the prototypes have been proven successful. The project aims eventually to build 100 exemplar homes at Freedom Park, a shack district on the outskirts of Cape Town.

In February 2007, work started on the first prototype home, designed by Cape Town architects MMA. This uses a construction system called EcoBeam, which involves stacking sandbags around a simple framework of timber struts strengthened with thin steel bars. The method requires no electricity and very little skilled labor, so people can build their own homes. The designers claim the sandbag walls are as strong and as thermally efficient as masonry, for a fraction of the cost.

Artek Pavilion

Date **2007**
Place **Milan, Italy**
Designer **Shigeru Ban**

Two Finnish companies and a Japanese architect came together in 2007 to build a demountable pavilion from innovative, sustainable materials. The Artek Pavilion, launched in Milan in April of that year, was commissioned by Finnish furniture brand Artek as a mobile venue for showcasing its products in a way that reflected the company's environmental concerns. The pavilion was designed by Japanese architect Shigeru Ban, who has pioneered the use of recyclable construction materials such as paper and cardboard (see page 232). For this project, Ban made substantial use of new composite materials developed by another Finnish company, the papermaking giant UPM.

Constructed in the form of an extruded house, the 131-foot-long (40 m) long building consists of a structural frame covered in cladding panels with a transparent section toward the center to allow natural light in, and it is open at both ends. The structural frame, internal surfaces, and flooring panels are constructed from a wood-plastic composite called UPM ProFi that is made of waste material from UPM's self-adhesive label–making business. The material, which consists of 70 percent paper and 30 percent plastic, can be extruded into structural components or fashioned into boards that can be worked in a way similar to wood. Tough and light, the material does not need to be sealed for outdoor use.

A plywood platform supports the pavilion, which consists of a run of twenty-one identical modular frames made of L-shaped ProFi extrusions. Originally developed as a corner-protecting material for UPM's own use, the product is here used structurally to create beams and cross-members that are joined together with steel plates. In all, 8.75 miles (14 km) of composite profiles are used in the 2,153-square-foot (200 sq m) building, which is 131 feet (40 m) long, 16 feet (5 m) wide, and 19.5 feet (6 m) high. The pavilion is designed to be dismantled easily and has been used to display Artek's products at design shows around the world.

Cardboard Bridge

Date **2007**
Place **Gardon River, France**
Designer **Shigeru Ban**

Japanese architect Shigeru Ban has pioneered the use of paper and cardboard as structural materials for the last twenty years, using these potentially renewable and recyclable materials to build houses, industrial units, exhibition venues, and most recently, a footbridge. The bridge, temporarily erected over the Gardon River in southern France in the summer of 2007, is not made entirely of cardboard, instead consisting of 281 cardboard tubes linked by steel connectors. The bridge's steps are made of recycled paper and plastic, while the foundations are made of sand-filled wooden boxes buried in the riverbanks rather than steel or concrete.

Ban began experimenting with industrial cardboard tubes in the 1980s, placing them side-by-side vertically to create partitions and walls, mixing these with more conventional structural systems in pioneering works such as the Miyake Design Studio Gallery in Tokyo (1994) and Paper House in Yamanashi, Japan (1995). Ban was instrumental in changing Japanese construction regulations to recognize cardboard as a legal building material in order to realize these projects. He later produced experimental temporary houses from paper tubes for people made homeless by earthquakes in Japan, Turkey, and India. These were completely recyclable, featuring foundations made of used beer crates filled with sand and made watertight with tarpaulin roofs.

In the late 1990s he developed a method of employing paper tubes as a structural material by creating giant arches constructed of lattices of short lengths of tubing held together with plywood bracings. His 1998 Paper Dome at Gifu, Japan, the first structure to be built this way, has an 88.5-foot (27 m) span and supports a roof of corrugated polycarbonate panels.

Ban's temporary Japan Pavilion at Expo 2000 in Hanover, Germany, was his most ambitious project to date and the largest paper structure ever built: a 243-foot-long (74 m), 82-foot-wide (25 m), and 52-foot-high (16 m) arched structure constructed of paper tubes. The complex "gridshell" form of the building, which curves in two directions and has undulating surfaces reminiscent of a caterpillar, was designed to contain the intense lateral forces experienced by the lattice of 5-inch (12.5 cm) diameter tubes. Ban worked with legendary German structural engineer Frei Otto—who pioneered the use of steel and timber gridshells—to perfect the highly advanced structure. German regulations forced Ban to compromise his structure by adding a timber substructure and plastic and metal elements to tie the structure together, but otherwise it was a highly sustainable building that featured a paper-and-fabric membrane roof and sand-filled foundations, meaning nearly every component could be recycled when the pavilion was dismantled.

Ban's exploration of cheap, reusable, off-the-shelf construction materials recently led him to design a demountable art gallery made of steel shipping containers. His Nomadic Museum was created to serve as the home of a traveling art exhibition. The 152 stacked containers that make up the museum have to date been erected in Venice; New York City; and Santa Monica, California.

Solar House Series

Date **2007**

Place **Washington, D.C.**

Designer **Darmstadt University of Technology**

The Solar Decathlon is a competition that invites colleges and universities to design and build solar-powered houses. Held in Washington, D.C. every two or three years, it aims to stimulate investigation into more energy-efficient homes and promote high design standards.

The overall winner of the 2007 Solar Decathlon was a design by Darmstadt University of Technology of Germany. Their rectangular, flat-roofed design (see facing page, bottom, for external view) won first place in all three judging categories—architecture, engineering, and lighting—and was also given a maximum score for its energy systems.

The building's envelope is arranged in layers, with each layer performing a different function. Outermost is a layer of wooden louver shutters that provide shade and privacy, while photovoltaics on the louvers generate electricity. The second layer provides insulation, with vacuum insulation panels (hollow panels from which all the air has been removed, which dramatically reduces heat convection) on the east and west façades, and quadruple-glazed floor-to-ceiling windows on the north and south. Both the shutters and the windows can be opened manually, opening the house to daylight and fresh air or sealing it for privacy and warmth. The third layer is the central core,

which contains the living elements and technical facilities. For flexibility, the interior of the house is configured in zones rather than rooms and features a double floor with panels that can be removed to provide living and sleeping spaces.

The house employs passive heating systems, with the sun providing most of the warmth required through the large south-facing windows and the high levels of insulation conserving warmth. As a result, it requires less than one-tenth of the energy needed to heat a typical German home. Other energy-saving techniques including the use of "phase-changing materials," or PCMs, in the windowless east- and west-facing walls. These are materials that change from solid to liquid when exposed to heat, drawing heat from the house that is later released when the air temperature cools. In this way they help stabilize interior temperatures. Many different PCMs can be used, including organic substances such as waxes and vegetable extracts.

Natural, locally grown materials are used where possible, with the prototype house made of German oak. The house is made of three equally sized modules that can be made in a factory and delivered on a truck.

World Mammoth and Permafrost Museum

Date **2007**

Place **Sakha-Yakutia, Siberia, Russia**

Designer **Leeser Architecture**

This project attempts to solve a familiar environmental conundrum: how to encourage public understanding of fragile ecosystems by allowing people to witness them firsthand without damaging them in the process. Permafrost is soil that remains at or below the freezing point all year round, creating a frozen crust that is typically up to 13 feet (4 m) deep. It covers around 20 percent of the earth's surface but as temperatures rise due to global warming, permafrost in Siberia and Alaska has been thawing at record rates. Scientists are concerned that melting permafrost could release large amounts of methane, which is a powerful greenhouse gas.

New York studio Leeser Architecture won an international competition in 2007 with their design for the World Mammoth and Permafrost Museum, which will be built directly on the fragile permafrost near the city of Yakutsk in the Russian republic of Sakha-Yakutia in Siberia. The purpose of the museum is to provide research facilities for scientists investigating this delicate but extremely harsh environment while simultaneously allowing members of the public to learn about both the ecosystem and the work of the scientists.

In order to minimize damage to the landscape and to prevent the transfer of heat to the frozen ground—which could melt the ice and cause the building to sink—the museum will be raised 20 feet (6 m) above the permafrost on tapering legs. The roof is covered in similarly tapering but inverted legs, which here act as light collectors. These are angled towards the south and west and funnel light from the low sun into the building. Photovoltaics and wind turbines will reduce dependence on the electricity grid while the building's translucent double-skinned exterior is filled with aerogel: a lightweight, semitransparent foam that has extremely good insulating properties.

Inside are gardens planted with native permafrost species such as grasses and lichens, which help purify the air and maintain humidity, while the building provides access to an underground gallery that displays the recently discovered body of a wooly mammoth.

Linked Hybrid

Date **2005**

Place **Beijing**

Designer **Steven Holl Architects**

As China modernizes, the country is building on a scale never seen before, expanding its cities and industries at an astonishing rate. With two new electricity-generating stations being built every week on average, and the nation's carbon dioxide emissions rising by around 9 percent per year, there are concerns over the environmental impact as a nation of 1.3 billion people constructs a modern infrastructure. Yet China is rapidly emerging as a country at the forefront of green design, with architects and designers working in the country being encouraged to incorporate the latest environmental thinking into their projects.

Linked Hybrid, by American architect Steven Holl, is a 15-acre (6 hectare) development of eight towers beside the old city wall in Beijing that will provide homes and facilities for 2,500 people when it is completed. Featuring one of the largest geothermal cooling and heating systems in the world, the development will be both heated and cooled by pumping water from 328 feet (100 m) below ground via six hundred wells drilled into the ground. The water will be pumped through the building's concrete floors, maintaining a steady temperature in both summer and winter. Geothermal heating and cooling systems make use of the heat found just below ground,

where temperatures tend to be steady all year round (50–86°F/10–30°C, depending on the local climate). In winter, pumps known as "ground-source heat pumps" extract this heat and transfer it to buildings. The pumps can save between 40 and 70 percent of the cost of heating a building, and 30 to 50 percent of the cost of cooling.

Linked Hybrid has other green features, including green roofs and gray-water recycling, but its most notable feature is the elevated pedestrian bridges that link the towers together. These contain cafés, gyms, and other facilities and are designed to reduce the need for residents to travel outside the development.

Masdar Initiative

Date **2006**
Place **Abu Dhabi, United Arab Emirates**
Designer **Foster + Partners**

The vast oil reserves found beneath the desert sands have made Abu Dhabi, the capital of the United Arab Emirates, one of the wealthiest cities on earth—and also one of the least sustainable, since the recent construction boom has created forests of skyscrapers heavily dependent on air-conditioning and desalinated water (a process that consumes vast amounts of energy). The inhabitants, meanwhile, are among the most car-dependent in the world, driving between buildings in climate-controlled gas-guzzlers.

Yet Abu Dhabi, aware that its oil will one day run out, is attempting to position itself as a leader in sustainable urban design. Announced in 2006, the Masdar Initiative (*masdar* is Arabic for "the source") is an ambitious research project that will investigate new energy-efficient processes. At its heart is a proposed 2.3 square-mile (6 sq km) campus in the desert close to Abu Dhabi that is billed by its architects, Foster + Partners, as the "world's first zero-carbon, zero-energy city."

The campus, which will host academic institutions, research facilities, and businesses, is based on ancient Middle Eastern planning principles, with the entire development nestled inside protective walls, a grid of car-free streets partially covered with screens to keep out the sun, and zoning designed to minimize the distance between people and amenities such as transport hubs and shops: nobody will be more than 656 feet (200 m) from public transportation. Buildings will be at most five storys high, with wind towers based on the local vernacular designed to funnel cooling desert breezes into the development.

Power will be supplied by a solar-powered plant with up to 80 percent of roof space in the city used for photovoltaics, while a personalized mass-transit system is being developed to reduce dependence on cars. Economically, the city aims to be at the forefront of new sustainable technologies, with a plant to manufacture advanced thin-film photovoltaic cells among the proposed industries.

Downland Gridshell

Date **2002**

Place **Sussex, England**

Designer **Edward Cullinan Architects**

This experimental building investigates ways of combining ancient building techniques, low-energy construction processes, and advanced computer-generated geometries. Designed by Edward Cullinan Architects, the Downland Gridshell is, as its name suggests, a gridshell structure. It is located at the Weald and Downland Open Air Museum in Sussex, England, which hosts a collection of restored historic timber buildings in a rural setting. The gridshell building, which is 39–49 feet (12–15 m) wide and two stories high, serves as a workshop for the museum's carpenters and craftspeople, while the basement is used for storage, administration, and exhibitions.

A gridshell is a lightweight, shell-like structure that curves in two directions but which is made of strips of material that crisscross each other in a grid rather than having a solid surface. Gridshells can be made of any material and have in the past been constructed of steel, aluminum, and even cardboard, but the Downland Gridshell is a pioneering structure made of "green" (unseasoned) oak laths. It was built by first assembling a double-layered flat lattice of slender oak struts on a raised scaffold. The wooden strips were joined together with fixings made of metal plates and bolts designed to allow the timber to flex in all directions. The edges of this grid were then bent down towards the ground to form a complex, self-supporting three-dimensional structure. The structure had first been extensively modeled on a computer to ensure it had sufficient rigidity to support itself and to withstand wind and rain. The roof's wavy shape—described by the designers as a "triple bulb hourglass" form—gives added rigidity along the length of the building.

The outside of the structure is clad in loose wooden shingles on the lower parts and sheets of glass higher up. The very top of the roof, which is more difficult to drain, is protected with a watertight cap. The building is designed to consume as little energy as possible. The high levels of natural light flooding through the glazed portions of the roof mean the building does not have to be artificially lit at all during the day. Rainwater is collected and heated by solar power, then pumped through the underfloor heating system. The basement is constructed with extremely thick walls to stabilize the temperature and create ideal conditions for preserving documents in the museum's archive.

National Assembly for Wales

Date **2005**
Place **Cardiff Bay, Wales**
Designer **Richard Rogers Partnership**

Designed as the home of the newly established Welsh parliament, this building was intended from the outset to be a standard-bearer for sustainable, inclusive design rather than yet another example of trophy architecture. Completed in 2005, it sits on Cardiff Bay, a natural harbor in the Welsh capital that was once the world's busiest coal-exporting port. With most of the nation's mines now exhausted or closed down, the construction of a low-energy building on the bay makes for a poignantly symbolic gesture.

The architects, Richard Rogers Partnership (now called Rogers Stirk Harbour + Partners), have long been at the vanguard of sustainable architecture, exploring ways of limiting energy consumption in buildings without compromising their unmistakable high-tech architectural language. For the National Assembly for Wales, the architects strived to reduce the environmental impact both of the materials used for construction and the resources required to run it after completion. The building uses local labor and materials where possible and is naturally ventilated to a large degree, with a 20-foot-high (6 m) rotating wind cowl atop the building. The cowl is inspired by those on traditional English oast houses, where hops used for making beer are dried. A timber funnel positioned above the debating chamber allows warm air to rise to the cowl, where it is dispersed. This and other natural ventilation systems prevents air-conditioning being required in the office areas of the building. The funnel is lined with a series of concentric aluminum rings, which reflect daylight into the chamber, reducing lighting requirements. A conical mirror located beneath the cowl reflects extra light from the low-lying winter sun. This mirror can be raised and lowered manually to adjust the levels of light it reflects.

The building also features a biomass boiler that burns wood chips to provide heat, while rain falling on the canopy-like roof is channeled inside steel columns to flush toilets, for cleaning purposes, and to irrigate the surrounding landscaping. The cost of running the building is claimed to be half that for a comparable building.

Norddeutsche Landesbank

Date **2002**

Place **Hanover, Germany**

Designer **Behnisch, Behnisch & Partner**

Glass is generally considered a poor material for use as architectural cladding in terms of its environmental performance, since glass-clad buildings tend to get cold in winter and hot in summer and require energy-intensive heating and cooling systems to keep them comfortable for workers. Yet corporations still insist on inhabiting glassy office towers, so architects are investing much thought into how to make such buildings greener. This office building in Hanover, Germany, headquarters for Norddeutsche Landesbank—the North German Clearing Bank—pulls out all the stops in its attempts to be environmentally friendly.

Designed by Stuttgart practice Behnisch, Behnisch & Partner, it contains a plethora of technologies intended to reduce energy consumption, including computerized blinds that adjust automatically according to the sun, natural ventilation (meaning, in this case, windows that can be opened manually), solar panels for water heating, and a geothermal system that uses water pumped from below ground to stabilize temperatures in the summer. The blocks have "green roofs" planted with sedum—a tough succulent—and wildflowers that absorb the sun's heat and prevent the building from overheating, while the open-air courtyard is brightened by a bank of heliostats, reflective panels that track the sun and bounce light into otherwise dark corners.

The unusual form of the building's central tower, which is seventeen stories high and features floors that shift in orientation and cantilever precariously, is partly the result of the designers having some fun—unusual with corporate clients—but also necessity, as German building regulations demand that workers' desks be no more than 20 inches (50 cm) from a window. Thus the narrow "fingers" of the tower shift to give each worker adequate daylight and are angled to maximize the amount of light falling into the courtyard.

Las Palmas Parasite

Date **2001**

Place **Rotterdam, Netherlands**

Designer **Korteknie Stuhlmacher Architecten**

With urban centers increasingly running out of development space and pressure to build in the countryside intensifying, many architects are looking for new ways to slot small green buildings into the city without requiring additional infrastructure. Underutilized rooftops are an obvious location for new structures such as this, and this temporary project, built on top of an elevator shaft atop a former warehouse in the Rotterdam docks, is a typical example of experimental "parasite" architecture.

Called Las Palmas Parasite after the building upon which it temporarily squatted, the building was designed by Dutch architects Korteknie Stuhlmacher Architecten as part of an exhibition on parasite architecture held in Rotterdam in 2001 during the city's European Capital of Culture celebrations.

Construction methods for the Parasite, which in this case stands for "prototype for advanced ready-made amphibious small-scale individual temporary ecological house," are extremely simple and flexible. The walls, floors, and roof of the 915-square-foot (85 sq m)

structure were constructed from solid laminated timber panels made of waste wood. All the panels were assembled and cut to size in an off-site factory and delivered flat-packed to save construction time on-site. The panels were left raw on the inside and covered with painted plywood on the outside, with irregular windows cut through the panels. All services, such as electricity and water, were supplied by the host building.

This particular building remained in place until 2005, when it was loaded onto a boat and sailed to a storage site, where it is awaiting a new location.

Other parasite projects include German designer Werner Aisslinger's Loftcube, a production design for a lightweight rooftop dwelling that can be craned onto an existing building to provide lodge-style accommodation; and the conceptual Rucksack Haus by German artist Stefan Eberstadt, which hangs on steel cables slung from the side of a building, providing additional accommodation that can be accessed through the windows of the host structure.

Lighthouse

Date **2007**

Place **Watford, England**

Designer **Sheppard Robson**

Like many countries, the U.K. is gradually introducing construction guidelines encouraging architects and builders to make future projects more sustainable. However, many large house-building companies seem reluctant to introduce green features, claiming they add to the cost or that there is little consumer demand for them. In order to generate debate about new housing and the environment, the U.K.'s Building Research Establishment held an event called Offsite 2007 to showcase green housing prototypes that offered viable alternatives to present volume-housing designs.

The prototypes all responded to the Code for Sustainable Homes, a voluntary assessment system introduced by the government in 2006 that rates houses on a scale of 1 to 6, with 6 applying to buildings that have zero carbon emissions. The event featured several prototypes designed by architects and built by house-builders, although the Lighthouse by Sheppard Robson for Kingspan Offsite was the only one rated as a zero-carbon-emissions building.

Lighthouse is a two-bedroom, two-and-a-half-story timber home with a steeply pitched roof creating high ceilings on the levels. Living areas are placed upstairs to take advantage of natural light provided by skylights, while bedrooms are downstairs. A "light funnel" on the roof channels natural light through the house and into the bedrooms. Energy efficiency is achieved via a raft of measures, including walls lined with highly insulated panels, passive cooling and ventilation systems, mechanical heat recovery systems, and photovoltaic panels on the roof.

Additional features that helped Lighthouse achieve its 6 rating include rainwater harvesting, gray-water recycling, and a system to prevent water runoff. Water runoff describes the situation when rainwater is channelled straight into the drainage system and removed rather than being allowed to soak into the ground. This contributes to the lowering of the water table in urban areas and can overload drainage systems and cause flooding during times of heavy rain. Lighthouse uses a "swell" to hold water until it can drain away naturally.

Index

Acknowledgments

The publishers would like to thank the following sources for their kind permission to reproduce the pictures in this book.

Key: t=Top, b=Bottom, c=Center, l=Left, and r=Right

1 Heath Nash; 2 Catherine Hammerton; 4 Liam Frederick; 5 TransGlass designed by Tord Boontje and Emma Woffenden; 6l Artek Studio; 6r and 7l Tom Dixon; 7r Artek Studio; 9 Atelier NL; 11 Christian Richters Photography

Lighting
12l Heath Nash; 12r Lovegrove Studio; 13 Tobias Wong/©Suck UK Ltd; 14–15 Come Rain Come Shine Light by Tord Boontje for Artecnica; 16 Tom Dixon; 17 Jason Bruges Studio; 18–19 Stuart Haygarth; 20 Gitta Gschwendtner; 21 Hulger; 22–23 Humberto and Fernando Campana, Transplastic 2007 Courtesy Albion; 24–27 Heath Nash; 28–29 Anke Weiss Studio; 30 Committee; 31–33 Lovegrove Studio; 34–35 Tobias Wong/©Suck UK Ltd; 36–37 Kennedy & Violich Architecture; 38 Potgerdesign; 39 ©Jakob Gade; 40–41 Olivia Cheung; 42–43 Demakersvan/©Igmar Cramers

Homeware
44l Christine Misiak; 44r Doshi Levien; 45l Alamy/©Coaster; 45r Atelier NL; 46–47 TransGlass designed by Tord Boontje and Emma Woffenden; 48–49 Arnout Visser; 50 TransNeomatic designed by Fernando and Humberto Campana for Artecnica; 51 Büro North; 52–53 Tomáš Gabzdil Libertiny/Studio Libertiny/©Raoul Kramer; 54 Muji; 55 Christine Misiak; 56–57 Alamy/©Coaster; 58–59 Mater/Thomas Ibsen; 60 Studio Jo Meesters; 61 Tom Dixon; 62–63 Karen Ryan; 64–65 Beads & Pieces designed by Hella Jongerius for Artecnica; 66 Doshi Levien; 67–69 Atelier NL

Furniture
70l Åbäke, www.gampermartino.com; 70r Jurgen Bey; 71l Russell Pinch; 71r Komplot Design; 72 Nendo; 73 Tatu designed by Stephen Burks for Artecnica; 74–75 Piet Hein Eek; 76 and 77r Emeco; 77l ©Nigel Young/Foster & Partners; 78–81 Artek Studio; 82–83 Komplot Design; 84–85 Artek Studio; 86; Vitra, www.vitra.com; 87–89 Maarten Baas/www.maartenbaas.com; 90 Johan Bruninx; 91 Russell Pinch; 92 Majid Asif; 93 Christian Kocx; 94–95 Ryan Frank; 96–97 Photos: Åbäke, www.gampermartino.com, Exhibition photos: Angus Mill; 98–99 Jurgen Bey; 100–101 Studio Lo; 102 Christopher Cattle; 103 Nina Tolstrup; 104–105 TAF Arkitektkontor

Textiles & Materials
106l Elsbeth Joy Nielsen; 106r Jelte van Abbem; 107l Photography by Erik Gould, Image courtesy of Museum of Art, Rhode Island School of Design; 107r Catherine Hammerton; 108–109 Pedrita; 110 Greetje van Tiem; 111l Photography by Pablo Mason, taken at the San Diego Museum of Contemporary Art as part of the Soundwaves exhibition 111r Photography by Erik Gould, image courtesy of Museum of Art, Rhode Island School of Design; 112–113 ©Ronan and Erwan Bouroullec; 114–115 Jelte van Abbema; 116–117 Greetje van Tiem; 118 Catherine Hammerton; 119 Elsbeth Joy Nielsen; 120–121 Gary Harvey

Products
122l Anton Gustafsson and Magnus Gyllensvärd; 122r Marks Barfield Architects; 123l Priestman Goode; 123r LOTS Design; 124 Galerie Rob Koudijs; 125 Emiliano Godoy; 126 Jack Godfrey Wood; 127 Anton Gustafsson and Magnus Gyllensvärd; 128–129 Scott Amron/Amron Experimental Inc; 130 Jule Jenckel; 131 www.atelierkg.com/Steven Kessels; 132 ©Marc Domage; 133 ©Véronique Huyghe; 134 Priestman Goode; 135 Levente Szabó/Electrolux; 136 Trevor Baylis; 137 Héctor Serrano; 138–139 DIY Kyoto; 140 Mathieu Lehanneur; 141 Ines Sanchez Calatrava/Ravensbourne College of Design and Communication; 142 Vestergaard Frandsen SA; 143 Pieter Hendrikse; 144–145 fuseproject; 146 Chauhan Studio; 147 Studio Leung; 148 Marks Barfield Architects; 149 Asif Khan; 150 Roelf Mulder; 151 Creative Review; 152 LOTS Design; 153 Alberto Meda/Miro Zagnoli

Transportation
154l Boeing Images; 154r Solarlab; 155 Seymourpowell; 156–157 JCDecaux; 158 Strida; 159 Nicolas Zurcher; 160–161 Seymourpowell; p162–163 Solarlab; 164–165 Studio Massaud; 166–167 Lovegrove Studio; 168 Tesla Motors; 169 Toyota (GB) PLC; 170 Honda; 171 Nuon Solar Team/Hans–Peter van Velthoven; 172 Loremo; 173–175 Boeing Images

Interiors
176 James Winspear; 177l Geoffrey Cottenceau; 177r Rita Cahill; 178–181 Steve Spiller; 182 Rita Cahill; 183tr&183b Pat Redmond; 183tl Rita Cahill; 184–185 James Winspear; 186–187 MIO; 188 Geoffrey Cottenceau; 189 ©Ronan and Erwan Bouroullec; 190–191 Caroline Pham/The New School; 192l and 193 Merkx + Girod architecten; 192r Roos Aldershoff; 194 Julia Lohmann; 195 Alexandra Jørgensen; 196–197 Mike Meiré; 198–199 Schemata Architecture Office; 200–201 Patrick Blanc

Architecture
202l Michael Freeman Photography; 202r Liam Frederick; 203l Sascha Kletzsch; 203r Christian Richters Photography; 204–205 Paul Smoothy; 206 Dennis Gilbert/View; 207 Sascha Kletzsch; 208 Richard Cooper; 209 Liam Frederick; 210–211 Gigaplex Architects; 212–213 www.zedfactory.com; 214–215 Christian Richters Photography; 216–219 Michael Freeman Photography; 220–221 C F Møller Architects, photographer Ole Hein Petersen; 222 MVRDV; 223 Pugh + Scarpa Architects; 224–225 Rob 't Hart fotografie; 226–227 Dennis Gilbert/View; 228–229 Rex Features/View Pictures/Paul Raftery; 230 Interactive Africa; 231 Shigeru Ban Architects Europe; 232–233 Didier Boy de la Tour; 234–235 www.solardecathlon.org; 236–237 Lesser Architecture; 238–239 ©Iwan Baan; 240–241 Foster & Partners; 242–243 ©Image Courtesy of Edward Cullinan Architects, Photographer Richard Learoyd; 244–245 Redshift Photography 2006; 246–247 Roland Halbe Fotografie; 248 and 249br Korteknie Stuhlmacher Architecten; 249tl, tr, bl Anne Bousema; 250–253 Hufton & Crow

Every effort has been made to acknowledge correctly and contact the source and/or copyright holder of each picture and North Atlantic Books apologizes for any unintentional errors or omissions, which will be corrected in future editions of this book.